Twelve Months to Your Daughter's Wedding

Twelve Months to Your Daughter's Wedding

by Sandra Krystal

iUniverse, Inc.
New York Lincoln Shanghai

Twelve Months to Your Daughter's Wedding

iUniverse, Inc.

For information address:
iUniverse, Inc.
2021 Pine Lake Road, Suite 100
Lincoln, NE 68512
www.iuniverse.com

ISBN: 0-595-32739-7 (pbk)
ISBN: 0-595-66678-7 (cloth)

Printed in the United States of America

Dedicated to my daughter Alexandra and son-in-law Adam
and
my loving partner Leonard

Contents

Preface

When my daughter, newly engaged, was asked if she needed a wedding planner, she quickly responded, putting her arm around my shoulder, "Oh, no, thanks; I have one. My mother." I blinked in amazement.

When she dreamily told me, "Oh, mom, I want a beautiful wedding with all the trimmings," I stared in disbelief.

My thoroughly Modern Daughter wanted a traditional wedding—with all the works! My pragmatic daughter who had a no-nonsense attitude and was forging a career at a major New York investment bank suddenly had stardust in her eyes as she outlined her vision of a fairy-tale wedding: a black tie affair with an 8-piece band, a string ensemble, champagne flowing and she whirling on the dance floor in a grand ballgown. My practical daughter, who had witnessed my struggle as I single-handedly brought up two children in Manhattan, sending them to private schools (how *did* I do it?), wanted a major wedding with a big sticker price. My undemanding daughter was now asking for her dream come true.

"Mom, I've always dreamed of a big wedding" caught me by surprise. My daughter? *My* daughter had always dreamt of a big wedding? Elation and guilt made my heart flutter and constrict at the same time. A parent cannot always make every dream come true for her child. I couldn't provide a father for her nor could I get her the perfect score she wanted on the SAT. I couldn't give her the two additional inches she wanted nor could I get her positioned well at Credit Suisse or Morgan Stanley but this request was possible. To make her a beautiful wedding was in my power and I was going to do my utmost to make this dream come true.

I started to envision the affair. I pictured my beautiful statuesque daughter with her long, white neck and upright carriage and I saw a Princess Bride in a flowing wedding gown. Under her veil, a demure visage, her alabaster skin softly dewy. I saw her groom, her soon-to-be-husband, Adam, walk towards her, arm outreached to take her hand in his and lead her to the altar and to a life of tender love.

The ceremony over, I saw my daughter smiling as she and her husband basked in congratulatory applause as they walked up the aisle to a trumpet extraordinaire. The picture in my mind was ephemeral, gauzy white with beautiful strains of soft, mellifluous music, like a magical scene from a mystical world akin to "A Midsummer's Night Dream." Everything was golden-toned and white silk, organza and tulle, sprinkled with twinkling lights, soft candles and molten melodies.

However, before this vision could be a reality, I had to plan it. Where to begin? Easy, I thought. I'd research the glut of bridal magazines (*Manhattan Bride, Bride, The Knot Wedding Pages*) and their respective websites, read some mother-of-the-bride books, get recommendations from my friends who had recently made weddings, hire the right people, and follow all the checklists.

I had no idea of the journey upon which I was embarking! Lists? Sure there are lists; there are myriad month-by-month lists to guide the novice wedding planner through every phase of the wedding—or so they appear. Until you actually start planning a wedding and realize these "lists" are so overwhelmingly filled with minutiae that they make wedding-planning seem the most daunting challenge one could ever face.

And the books that claim to be guides to making a beautiful wedding have seemingly been written by people who never planned for a real wedding. One advises hiring a DJ instead of a band simply because hiring a band means feeding the band members. Another, when addressing the expense of a wedding, advises that the bride or mother-of-the-bride pick up the flowers the day of the wedding, to save some money. This author, it is clear, has never experienced a wedding first-hand or she would never have made such a bizarre suggestion. When might the bride pick up the flowers—before she gets into her wedding gown or after?

This book will strongly advise hiring a live band, as nothing is as beautiful as in-the-flesh musicians playing great dance music. The fact that you have to feed the band members is irrelevant; it is the cost differential that will be the deciding factor between hiring one DJ as opposed to a six or eight or ten-piece band.

Moreover, nothing—no lists, nothing that's out there in print, no amount of research, no article or book, no advice from friends who have done this before—prepares you for the indescribable, ineffable experience of planning your daughter's wedding. Yes, it's about getting a venue, hiring a band, a photographer and a florist. Yes, it's about gowns and dresses and tuxedoes and hairstyles and guest lists and food selection. When all is accomplished and every detail attended to you learn that it is about much more.

It's about feelings that run the gamut from joy to sadness, from love to anger, from stress to self-praise—often all in one day! One moment you feel a great loss and are overtaken by a heavy sadness; the next minute you are elated; suddenly, you are crying; and often you are too exhausted for any emotion at all. Nothing can prepare you for the emotional tsunamis you'll experience.

When I began my role of Wedding Planner, I was naïve and, therefore, quite sure I'd pull it off with aplomb. What was all the hysteria about when women told me about planning their daughter's wedding? What was wrong with them? Had they never made a big party before?

And I was a terrific planner. After all, it was part of my business background—working with Events Managers at New York hotels overseeing parties for directors of foundations, planning celebratory luncheons for 500 teenagers, directing major fund-raising events and heading up the yearly auction at *The New Lincoln School*, a private school that my son had attended.

I knew how to motivate people. I knew how to enlist people to volunteer their time for good causes. For one auction, I convinced Philip de Montebello to take the highest bidder on a private showing of the highlights of the *Metropolitan Museum of Art* and then lunch with that bidder in the membership dining room. When I was vice-president of an educational organization, I persuaded Peter Jennings to be the Master of Ceremonies at a luncheon attended by 400 New York City school-children and to assist me in bestowing awards to those who had performed outstanding service in their communities. I lectured, conducted workshops at national conferences and oversaw grant programs in five states across the United States. Certainly, I knew how to plan, how to execute and how to mobilize people.

The horror wedding stories detailing arguments and conflict—with the florist, the band, the bride, the groom, the future in-laws!—would not occur with this wedding. No such confrontations would involve me and mine. There would be no arguments with my daughter, no differences with my future son-in-law and absolutely no conflicts with his parents. I knew all the possible minefields and I would ensure that there were no mines!

Beware the hubris of thinking you can pull it off—a perfect wedding. Nothing is perfect. No wedding has taken place without some minor glitch or even a major mishap. My friend's daughter was saying "I do" when she heard a thud behind her. When she turned around, there was her maid of honor passed out on the floor! There are grandmothers who fall, microphones that don't work, wedding gowns that aren't finished on time and, horror of all horrors, grooms who don't show up for the affair! The most experienced wedding planner cannot foresee every possible mishap.

But you can ensure that your daughter has a beautiful wedding if you know beforehand the possible pitfalls. The process of planning and decision-making can be less complicated, if you are guided correctly. Because I didn't have such guidance, I made errors, wasted time, had to remake decisions, redo some planning and re-evaluate priorities.

The purpose of this book is to prevent you from experiencing mishaps, detours and delays. This book, filled with practical and worthwhile advice, takes you through the twelve months of preparations, guiding you each month along the way so you can achieve making your daughter's dream come true.

Introduction

Since there cannot be a Perfect Wedding, your more realistic goal might be to make a beautiful wedding, a wonderful wedding, a dream come true. To accomplish this all you need to do is follow a few precepts. They are:

Simplify

Chunk down

Know that no matter what your decision, it will be fine.

Oh, if I can fully convey the meaning of these simple statements.

It is so important to understand that everything will be wonderful, no matter what decision is made. If you decide to make the wedding on a Saturday in June or a Sunday in March, it will be fine. If the mother-of-the-bride decides to wear a black silk strapless or a beige spangled ballgown, it will look fine. If the bride selects a jewel-encrusted bodice or a simple satin A-line, she will look beautiful. If you have a twelve-piece orchestra or a solo DJ, people will dance. If the officiant mumbles and bungles his speech or chants majestically, he or she will marry your daughter to her groom. If the food is not sensational, people will eat. They have come to witness a wedding ceremony and partake in the joy of the event. If the wine flows and the music plays, they will have memories of a wonderful wedding.

In order to simplify, you must have a closed mind. What I mean is—*decide first and then look.* If you are going to have an open mind to all possibilities, you are going to burden yourself with myriad options that will just create angst and take away from the pleasure that planning a wedding should be about.

There are many aspects in planning a wedding but the major issues that can pose the most challenges and/or disagreements are the following:

The wedding list: Deciding upon the amount of people to invite to your wedding will be in direct correlation with the amount of money that you plan to spend. You must have a good idea of the budget. This will enable you to develop a guest list that synchronizes with the total cost of the wedding. If you select a venue,

1

which is just one item in the total budget, that charges $350 per person, perhaps you don't need 200 attendees!

The venue: Narrow it down immediately by deciding upon the locale. How far or near from your home will you have it? If the bride and groom are from different cities or states, decide in which city or state the wedding will take place and then look close to that home. Will you have the ceremony and the dinner/dance in the same place or will you have the ceremony in a place of worship and the reception and dinner somewhere else?

The invitations: Before looking at samples that confuse and frustrate, decide upon the kind of invitation you want. Do you want something traditional? Funky? Modern? When you are sure of your preference (and stick to your decisions!), then look at the sample invitation books. And keep these at a minimum. Three is the magical number.

The wedding dress: Women have a good idea of their figure and know what they look good in. To begin your research, simply start looking through magazines to get ideas. Start collecting pictures of gowns you like. Then start exploring bridal salons. Again, I would suggest staying close to home and exploring no more than six. Anything beyond six salons and all the gowns start looking alike.

However, before budgets and venues and wedding gowns, there is the beginning, the prelude.

PART I
Prelude

There is much that leads up to a wedding. There is the story of the way the bride and groom met, their falling in love and their becoming engaged. There is the selection of the engagement ring and, perhaps, an engagement party. There is the meeting of the families who suddenly have a tremendous connection through their daughter and son. A few months before the wedding, there might be another party to plan—the bridal shower.

A little-discussed aspect of things that lead up to a wedding is feelings. The feelings you experience when your daughter comes home and announces she has fallen in love. The shock you experience when you realize that you are losing your daughter. There are the memories of your falling in love and your wedding day and the feelings that are elicited from these reminiscences. These emotions brought up from deep in your psyche as you begin to recall past events in your life can be overwhelming.

1

My Mother, My Daughter and Me

After picturing my daughter's wedding—in which Adam comes to lead her, all beauty and grace, to the *chuppa* and to a life of devotional love—I recalled a similar scene from my wedding. There I was, turning to the congregation as Mendelssohn's "Wedding March" announced that I was Mrs. Herbert Krystal. My husband, turning with me, handsome in his top hat, was grinning as broadly as I. Such a handsome couple we were. Oh, the elation I had felt at that moment as everyone applauded, congratulating us on this special occasion. I was so filled with joy and hope and had such a beautiful vision of my future. Unbeknownst to me at that moment in time, we would divorce 12 years later. What would cause the dissolution of my marriage? Oh, nothing more than a basic ignorance about whom I was marrying.

A young girl, coming of age in the Bronx in the 1950s, simply knew that she had to get married—preferably to a doctor or a lawyer. These professions were identifiable to our Jewish mothers; these professions would provide us with a comfortable life style and would add status to the clan.
"My son-in-law, the doctor," would be my mother's boast. And eyebrows would rise.

However, the qualities these doctors and lawyers should possess were a complete mystery to us. All we knew was that they should be good looking and if not rich yet easily on the way. So Sheila married her doctor and Diane married her doctor and Marcia married her lawyer. I took a few more years before I landed mine. I was 29 when Mendelssohn's melody announced me as the Doctor's wife.

My daughter, coming of age in Manhattan in the 1990s, is a sophisticated young woman, greatly informed and certainly knowledgeable about the qualities a husband should possess. In my generation daughters were told to marry a doctor, while in today's world daughters are told to be one. Moreover, I couldn't have had any pre-conceived notions of what path my daughter's life should take, as she has a mind very much her own. I reared her that way.

At two, when I saw her playing with blocks creating a corral encircling little animals, I immediately sat down and redirected her play, helping her to build a tall tower. My daughter was not going to be typecast as a nurturer, a womb-builder. Like her two-year old male counterparts, she, too, could lift off into space and fly. At three, when her nursery-school teacher brushed her off, my daughter announced, one hand on her hip, "You know when you talk to me that way it hurts my feelings!" When it was time for a private high school, I selected an all-girl school so she would learn that she could be the captain of the team, the president of the debate club or the CEO!! For Alexandra to tell people what she wanted was second-nature to her. Unlike her mother who couldn't talk up and ask for sprinkles on her ice-cream cone, Alexandra let you know when she wanted a whole ice-cream cake. But she does it in the most charming way.

Thinking about making a grand wedding for my daughter stirred up memories of my wedding to her father, so long ago. I rummaged around on the shelf of my coat closet, the one with all the picture albums that attest to every significant event in my life, until I found it—an old, white leather (a little yellowed now) album inscribed in gold—"Sandra and Herbert—December 14, 1969." There I was in a Juliet-style wedding dress with rows of tiny pearls on the bodice and a pearl-encrusted tiara capping my head. And there was my mother, rather attractive in her pale, yellow lace gown, her hand on my arm quite content with her daughter's accomplishment.

My mother was so excited about "Our Wedding," as she referred to it. Her strong identification with my nuptials was quite symbolic of our relationship which was one of intense symbiosis. I was making her dream come true by marrying the doctor she hadn't—a young man who was attending medical school. When I was a little girl, she would show me letters from him and a picture of a handsome young man in a raccoon coat, leaning on a roadster, quite dashing and self-assured.

"I was a greenhorn," she would say, "and he was from a wealthy family."

So, although she never talked to me about boys or relationships and definitely not sex (she seemingly had three children by Immaculate Conception!), I knew one thing—I was to marry a doctor.

My mother had had no idea about marriage. All she knew was that she didn't feel she was good enough for her Doctor and when she met my father at the Strawberry Festival, she was terribly attracted to him.

"He was very sure of himself," she told me. "He took me by surprise."

I can hear him telling her with his brawny bravado, "Dance with anyone you want but save the last dance for me. I'm taking you home at the end of the night."

And he walked away, leaving her on her own and then, as promised, claimed her at the end of the night.

"I felt safe with him," she confessed to me.

But they were such different people, different sensitivities, different dreams, different natures—they truly should never have married.

The concept of opposites attracting is not the basis for a good relationship. My mother, demure and shy, had initially been attracted to my father's outgoing nature and his macho ways. Too soon, she became jealous of his flirtatious manner and repulsed by his down-to-earth dynamism. She became Blanche to his Stanley, even to the undershirt at the dinner table on hot summer nights. Her virginal ways clashing with his raw sexuality caused battles and minor skirmishes between them for 66 years.

"What did I know?" she would say. "All my mother could advise me was to follow my heart."

Her legacy was that I, too, knew nothing about marriage. But in my day, divorce was an option. And did I use it! When I was 23, my mother, distraught that I wasn't yet married and frightened that her daughter would be an *old maid*, talked only of marriage. So I accommodated her and married the first guy to come along one Labor-Day weekend that had come on the heels of a disappointing summer. He walked up to me, as I was washing my little blue Fiat in front of my building on Sheridan Avenue, in the Bronx, and asked me out. Three months later, I awoke one morning—married and stunned. It took me a year before I flew to Tijuana to appear at a Mexican courtroom to obtain divorce papers written in

Spanish on pale-gold parchment folded and sealed with red wax. Since I couldn't read it, I simply trusted my lawyer to confirm that I was divorced.

Then I married the Doctor. Tall, dark and handsome (weren't these the important traits?), he was my mother's dream come true. It turned out, however, that he really didn't like being a doctor so instead of going to his office, he frequented art galleries on Madison Avenue (I had made it to Manhattan!) A therapist explained what a passive-aggressive was and advised me, "You're young and attractive; divorce him and try again."

At 41, divorced with two young children and still clueless as to what to look for in a mate, I re-entered the dating scene. One man only saw me on the week-ends that I didn't have my children, and he coldly explained, "No man gets up in the morning hoping he'll meet a middle-aged woman with two children."
"Good-bye, Tom."
Another, in deep analysis exploring his relationship with his primal caretaker, announced one day that he couldn't see me anymore. "To date you is to deny my mother," he said. I didn't care to have this explained!
"Good-by Dick."
A third questioned why I wasn't an expert tennis player. I spewed, "While you were perfecting your serve, I was bring up two children single-handedly." That certainly didn't go over well and I never heard from him.
"Good-bye Harry."

So when Mort came along, ten years older than me and riddled with diabetes offering to love not only me but also my little girl (men find teen-age boys hard to love if they're not their own), I jumped at the opportunity. He snapped his fingers, *a la* the magician (which was his avocation) and whatever we wished for came true. He created a fantasy life spoiling Alexandra and me for the next three years until he died.

Undaunted, I married once again (who was counting?) when I fell in love with Leonard. Alexandra was 16 years old when she witnessed her mother's fourth marriage so she had had a lot of first-hand experience. She had witnessed a lot. She knew what qualities to look for in a man and knew when she met Adam that he had every requisite and then some.

2

Madam, I'm Adam: Meeting the Future Son-in-Law

What if your daughter comes home and tells you she is in love? What would you say or do? First, you would probably listen and let her tell you all about him—how they met, what he looks like, what he does, why she fell in love with him, etc. Then, if you're like me, you will want to meet him. And you pray that you'll like him, too.

At 24, Alexandra was just starting out to carve a career, so she stunned me one night by announcing, "Mother, God has sent me an angel and I have the good sense to recognize it."

I hadn't even known that she was dating, let lone falling in love. But she hadn't really known either; it happened so fast. A friend at work had pronounced one day, "You have to meet my brother. You two are going to hit it off." And that is exactly what happened. Her friend arranged for the three to meet for a drink: herself, her brother, Adam, and Alexandra.

After two drinks, as Alexandra was exiting and saying good-night (she had an appointment with me to see a movie), she tripped and fell flat on her face. "He's never going to call me, mom." she moaned when we met up later, "I was such a *klutz*. I tripped right over a chair!"
I was upset that she had ended their meeting just to keep our appointment.
"You could have called me and told me what was happening. I didn't need to see a movie tonight."

But she, often quite wiser than her mother, explained, "No, mom, it's better this way. This way, if he liked me, it's more intriguing that I had to leave for another appointment." Still, she was concerned about her unglamorous exit and was afraid he wouldn't call.

Obviously, love had struck simultaneously for he did call and on their first date Adam asked, "I don't want to rush you but can we be exclusive?"

And so, one night, when I was reading in bed, my daughter came home from her first date and told me about the angel that had been sent to her. My daughter, at 24, was in love. I cannot describe the emotion that swept through my body. The elation, the fear, the startling knowledge of my loss. My little girl, this beautiful innocent under a sophisticated veneer, was now going to enter into a relationship with a man. She was going to love a man and have the joy of a loving relationship. She was now going to love another. With a dull awareness, I was realizing the dawn of my daughter's new life and simultaneously feeling the void it would create in mine.

I quickly remembered that "you don't lose a daughter; you gain a son." So I thought about meeting Adam. Twice the doorman rang up and Alexandra ran down to meet him in the lobby of our building. Suddenly, I, who had been through four weddings and a funeral, became my old-fashioned parents.
"Let them know that you have parents who are concerned about you. Make them come up to the apartment to pick you up," my father had advised.

So, I suggested one night, "Let him know that you have a mother who is concerned about you. I think you should have him come to the apartment to fetch you." I even used the word fetch!! What was happening to me? Of course, I reassured her that all I would say was, "Hello Adam, how nice to meet you."
"Don't you dare say anything else mom," she warned. "Nothing like—'Oh Alexandra has told me so much about you.' And don't you dare ask him anything about himself or his family."

After she issued these dire warnings, Adam came to the door and I stood there mute. Then I extended my hand and stupidly said, "Hello Adam how nice to meet you." Alexandra swiftly arrived at our entranceway and gave me a wisp of a kiss good-bye and whisked him out the door.

My daughter is a very level-headed young woman. So, although I wondered how she could have fallen in love so swiftly, I knew she was listening to both her heart and her head. And there was a lot in that pretty head of hers. Alexandra knew what requisites a young man needed in order to win her heart. And, she explained to me, Adam had them all. She enumerated some: charm, intelligence, sensitivity to others' needs, perceptivity, wit and, yes, good looks. Her heart spilled over as she told me, "He has goals, mommy, and a solid idea of what he wants from life. And he has a wonderful code of ethics."

They had discussed their careers and she apprised me that, "To be successful in his career is critical to him but it doesn't mean he has to step on other people to achieve it. He has principles." Alexandra gushed with enthusiasm, "We want to do the same things; we have the same interests, the same dreams—and he loves me very much."
This sounded good to me.

I wanted to know this young man who had won my daughter's heart so I suggested dinner. Alexandra agreed.
"Where should I make the reservation?" I asked, excited that I'd be spending an entire evening with them.
"Mom, we're both vegetarians, you know, so make sure the restaurant has vegetable dishes."
"How about a fish restaurant?" I asked.
"Mom, we're vegans."

Vivolo, on Lexington Avenue, promised a delicious vegetarian dinner. As we three walked up the avenue I, walking quickly in animated conversation, turned toward them for a response to what I was saying—but they weren't there. I turned my head further and saw them a half block behind, walking in a steady, stolid pace. I watched my daughter and her beaux, two tall, handsome young people, and was struck by the picture they presented. Both walking at their *kapha* pace; they were a perfect match. And I chuckled as I remembered that *kaphas,* cautious and steady, are also sensuous and wise. I sighed contentedly. This union was a good one, I concluded.

I waited for them to catch up to me and then slowwwly we continued our walk up the avenue and by the time we reached the restaurant, I had fallen in love, too. This charming young man was not charming me; he was simply charming. Yes, Alexandra, had found an angel and we were blessed. She because she would have the most devoted and loving man at her side forever; I, because I knew that my daughter would be loved and would have her dreams come true.

Dinner was filled with bright conversation and he was more delicious than the food. He spoke with wit and listened with earnestness; he smiled and laughed. He had great sincerity, warmth and glowed with goodness. I knew immediately why my daughter had fallen so in love with him. He was the most special young man I had ever met in my entire life.

After a resoundingly successful dinner, the next step was for my daughter to meet his parents.

3

Country Mouse, City Mouse

My daughter was in love with "the most wonderful person G-d ever created" to use her exact words.

"He's everything I could ever have wanted," she proclaimed.

There was only one immediate difference that I saw. They had been brought up in very different milieus.

When they met, Adam was a product of suburbia, specifically Cherry Hill, New Jersey and his family consisted of two parents, three siblings, two dogs and a horse. Alexandra was born and raised in Manhattan, the Upper East Side, and her family consisted of one mother and one brother.

Alexandra knew good things. When she was 8 years old, Mort had bought her a white rabbit fur coat and a brown fur jacket because she just couldn't decide which one she preferred. She accompanied us to dinner at *Lutece*, cruised with us to Nova Scotia and learned about compound interest. Although he died when she was eleven, he had given her an excellent foundation in appreciating the good life and it was part of who she was. When she went off to Colgate University, in her luggage were sweater sets (which she wore with a strand of pearls), fur hats and high-heeled boots. She knew *Saks Fifth Avenue* and *Bergdorf Goodman* and by the time she met Adam, she knew that a Fendi or a Prada was a basic must.

Adam, at 30, had just moved into the city from Cherry Hill. Before he could experience the Big City he had met Alexandra and his fate was set. He knew *Target*, *Ikea* and, at best, *Macy's*. Fendi probably sounded like a sports car to him. So Alexandra had a lot to teach him about what was *dernier cri*.

But these "differences" were deemed superficial. She knew the mettle from which Adam was made. Going full steam ahead, they planned on a week-end in Cherry

Hill for her to meet his parents, Dr. and Mrs. Barry Hoffman. When the big week-end arrived my only advice was, "Sweetheart, just be yourself."

Of course, I wasn't sure which self she should be. Alexandra is sweet and good and kind and generous and charming and sedate. She is also secure, assertive, opinionated and honest. Sometimes these can conflict. But I have never seen her not handle a situation with élan and equanimity. And I had no concern that the week-end would be anything but successful. A boy like Adam didn't just happen; he had to have had role models. Obviously, they were his parents.

But when Alexandra called me from work on Monday, I heard the strain in her voice and I became alarmed.

"Mom, I'll never live in suburbia! I thought I'd lose it out there. All we did was eat—the entire week-end was about food and I took a ride with Adam's mother to *Home Depot*."

I wasn't sure what *Home Depot* was but it didn't sound too exciting.

"Don't worry sweetheart, you only visited them; you don't have to live there."

"But mom, if that's where Adam grew up, that's what he obviously loves. I'd suffocate, mom, if I ever had to live outside the city. I need the city—the pace, the convenience, my GYM!" She was definitely in a panic in which I had never known her to be.

"Slow down, sweetheart. Did you talk about any of this to Adam?"

"Not yet. I have to digest it all and think it through first."

That sounded more like my analytical daughter.

I don't know how the discussion went, but in a week's time, again finding me reading in bed, she told me, her voice quivering with emotion, "Oh, mom, Adam said he would never do anything that would make me unhappy. Oh, mommy, (now she literally was crying), no one has ever said that to me before. I'm so lucky. He's so wonderful."

My daughter was definitely in love!

A week later, after clearly-stated conversations with him, she reported to me, "Adam said he loves the city and only wants to live here. What we both want when we are married is a week-end house in upstate New York. But we want to live and work here in the city."

My head started to pulse and my heart pounded or was it the other way around? I couldn't fully take it in at once. Did my daughter say "when we're married?" My heart tightened and I wasn't sure if I were excited or terrified, elated or sad. So I cried. I don't even remember if I blubbered something or just sat with the tears streaming down my cheeks. I do remember that I put my arms around her and held her so tight for so long.

4

Meeting the Family

Okay, you've met the young man who will be making your daughter's dreams come true. And they are talking very seriously and making plans for the rest of their lives. Depending upon the age of your daughter and whether she lives near you or across the country, the next step might be to meet the young man's family. Wanting everything to be "proper" and traditional, my daughter and her beaux wanted the families to meet. They were so excited.

"You'll love them, mom," Alexandra assured me.

It was I who had trepidations.

At this point, Adam's "traditional" family still consisted of one set of parents, three siblings, two dogs and a horse. However, Alexandra's family "picture" had recently changed. It now consisted of a mother, a brother, and a mother's ex-husband who had re-entered their lives. Leonard from whom I had been divorced for three years recently returned, declaring that he could not live any longer without me. This time, we decided to just live together; marriage was extraneous at this point, to say the least.

It is quite challenging when two families, strangers to one another, are suddenly thrust together because their children have fallen in love and are to marry. How do they find commonalities? Were we now, at the age of 50 plus, to make new friends? At nineteen it was hard enough for me to have friendships with girls. Now after five and a half decades of forming my personality and developing specific interests, I was to forge a friendship with a woman that my daughter was introducing me to because this woman was the mother of the man she was going to marry. Huh?

And to find common ground with Leonard and me is not easy. We have nothing in common with the thousands of golf players in our age category. We do not play tennis; nor do we ski. We like ideas and concerts and books and discussing politics. We like foreign films and the theatre and more books and more ideas. We are city folk through and through and the concept of suburbia has always frightened me.

"What do they do every day?"
I wondered about people who lived in single-family houses surrounded by trees and other single-family houses and who shopped in a mall a few miles away from an old town center. I've enjoyed week-ends in the country visiting some of these small towns on a picturesque fall day but I could never imagine living there day after day.
"You mean you have to get into the car to go for a container of milk?" I asked my sister when she married and moved to New Jersey. I was only sixteen.
When I moved to Manhattan right after college, I really couldn't imagine what people did in suburbia.
"Where are the boutiques?" I'd ask. "Where are all the restaurants?" I'd query.
"Where are the museums?" I wondered as I thought about the Metropolitan Museum that lifted my spirits higher with each step up the marble stairs of the stately building with its Corinthian columns. I couldn't imagine bringing up children without the Museum of Natural History right across town.
"What do suburbanites do every day?" I still wondered.

"Barbara loves horses," Alexandra informed me.
I looked at her with desperation. Horses?
"What will I talk to her about?"

Perhaps Alexandra was concerned as well. What would her thrice-divorced urbane mother talk about with Adam's suburban mother who had lead a comparatively sheltered life as the wife of the local doctor?

Her solution was a simple one. "Don't worry, mom. We're all going out to dinner. I've arranged it all."

The family meeting would occur in the Big City. The restaurant would accommodate all the varied tastes—well, almost. When she was told that Adam's brother Todd had found religion and an orthodox community in Munsey, New York, she had to make sure the restaurant was *kosher.*
"*Glatt* kosher, mom," Alexandra delineated.

"What's the difference between kosher and *glatt* kosher?" I asked.
No one seemed to know.

But Alexandra is excellent with *Google* searches. So, on a cold but sunny Sunday in January, under the guise of celebrating Adam's birthday, the two families dined at *Va Bene*, a well-known kosher restaurant on the Upper East Side. Ten people ate *glatt* kosher because Todd had found God. The menu boasted Italian fare but somewhere in the process of being blessed by a rabbi the food had lost a great deal of its taste.
"Oh, delicious," we all murmured.
"Umm, tasty," I gulped.
"Ma, what the heck is this I'm eating?" Jason whispered.
"I don't know, dear. Just smile."

Just about the time dessert was served, my son Jason, who is usually very diplomatic and extremely charming, was involved in a heated conversation with Todd about finance. As their voices neared crescendo, I prayed that my son would not go into his debate mode which entailed a battery of questions posed in rhetorical explosions. As if this weren't enough for my frayed nerves, Leonard, usually quiet in social situations, excused himself and left the restaurant. This act of egression created a silence, and ended even Jason and Todd's debate. I sat there with a pasted smile. Where the hell did he go? And was he coming back? Imagine my relief when he returned five minutes later with a *Kodak* instamatic.

There we were, two families meeting for the first time and Leonard returns with a camera. Plunging right in, I decided to fill the awkward silence with an activity. Of course, I completely forgot that my daughter had told me the Hoffmans were not a demonstrative family who certainly did not make public demonstrations of their affection. I forgot that she had told me of Adam's initial discomfort when she kissed him in public.

Suddenly, I heard a voice declare, "Everyone has to turn to the person on his or her right and kiss them." I was startled when I realized it was my own voice. For a split second, everyone stared. But when they began to comply, laughter warmed the frigid air and I clicked the camera. "Barry, you have to turn to Barbara and kiss her," I directed. Then Barbara turned to her right and kissed her son Todd. There was kissing all the way down the line or, rather, around the table. Everyone was laughing seemingly enjoying the tumult except my daughter who was sitting frozen, aghast, eyes wide in shock.

"Now Alexandra has to kiss Adam," I said, hoping to erase the terror on her face.

Toasts were then proclaimed. Happy birthday toasts to Adam. Toasts to the meeting of the clans. Toasts to all the young people seated around the table. Then Adam stood up and made a toast, "To Alexandra's mom, the Toast of the Town!"

5

The Engagement: A Crash Course in Diamonds, Part I

Soon after you have met your future son-in-law's family, the buzz will be engagement. And, of course, engagement rings! This is one aspect in which the mother-of-the-bride probably has the minimal amount of input. Young women today know what they want and few leave it up to their boyfriends—or their mothers. The selection of the engagement ring will probably be a shared decision between the young people.

Perhaps there are some young men who purchase a ring and surprise their girl-friends but when it comes to engagement rings, I really don't think the girl wants to be surprised. After all, a diamond ring is a major item she will be wearing the rest of her life.

Well, at least my daughter was not going to stay on the sidelines in this matter. She started her research. And this one went beyond Google! Short of taking a plane to Antwerp to its main diamond showroom on the tree-lined De Keyserlei to learn directly from the supplier, she researched on her own and learned everything there is to know about diamonds. She became more expert than my girl-friend's husband who has been a diamond dealer all his life. As a result of her intensive research, I knew she probably could pass the gemologist exam.

"The aspects that one looks for when purchasing a diamond are: color, shape, grade of cut and clarity," Alexandra explained to me. Alexandra had learned the alphabet color-coding system and knew a diamond rated D is absolutely color-less, very rare and very costly. She also learned that diamonds ranked E, F, G and H are colorless to the trained eye and she knew that when a diamond is mounted even J and K diamonds can look colorless but she could not be fooled.

She learned about the *American Gem Society Laboratories* that issues a Diamond Quality Document which is a document of authenticity.

"They list all the features of your diamond," Alexandra explained, "the shape and the style, the measurements and proportions, the grade of cut, the color and clarity—all are rated from zero to ten with zero being the most rare."

She learned about cut and polish and symmetry which effects how light enters and exits the diamond.

"It's all about brilliance," Alexandra began. "The most beautiful grade, mom, is ID for ideal, then comes EX for excellent, and VG for very good."

It sounded like my grading system when I marked my students' term papers, but I didn't mention this to Alexandra.

She learned about clarity and was able to discern any inclusions even between a VS1 and a VS2.

"I can forget about VVS1 and VVS2, mom; you can't even see an inclusion with a 10x magnifying glass so they're very costly," Alexandra reported. "But I'll be happy with a VS1 or VS2 which have inclusions that are not visible to the naked eye."

"People will not be looking at your engagement ring through a jeweler's loop," I assured her.

Secretly, I began to wonder about the three-carat ring I had stashed in my safe deposit box and made a mental note to look into it one day soon. I, unlike my daughter the researcher, had been dazzled when her father proposed and gave me a ring I had not known I was getting.

But I was concerned about her strong input into the selection of her engagement ring and expressed it to my son.

"Welcome to the 21st century," my son exclaimed. "No girl gets engaged these days without having a major role in selecting a ring she's going to wear for the rest of her life—or until a divorce."

"Thanks Jason," I said, "you're very encouraging."

When I thought I had learned all there was to know, she then explained color.

"But diamonds have no color, unless you're going to buy a yellow diamond," I stated with hesitation, knowing immediately that I was wrong.

So, I had another lesson coming. This lesson had to do with fire.
"The less color in a diamond, the more colorful the fire and the better the color grade," Alexandra said.

And again she explained the alphabet coding system that gives a D to an absolutely colorless stone, an E to a colorless stone that has only a minute trace of color which no one can see but an expert, and F that has slight color which, again, cannot be discerned by anyone but an expert in gems and G-H which is near-colorless.

I marveled at my gemologist who further investigated cuts and carats and decided upon the round, the 58 facet brilliant cut. Then she called my girlfriend's husband, told him exactly what she was looking for and when she went to his showroom with Adam, she demonstrated her knowledge flawlessly and I imagine that both my girlfriend's husband and Adam were floored.

Adam had three stones from which to select. He was a little taken aback with their size.
But Alexandra explained, "Adam, I'm a big girl and have long fingers; I need a big stone."
"For a stone that size, I need some time," Adam gulped.

Undaunted, he was not changing his mind at all; he just needed time to digest this new venture and see how he could come up with such capital.
"Mom, I'm doing the right thing, aren't I?" Alexandra asked. "A diamond is a good investment but only if the stone is at least three carats."
Who am I to disagree with this diamond maven. She has enough knowledge to be a member of the 47th Street Diamond Cutters Association.

Alexandra is a patient young woman.
"I don't want the ring in February because that's Valentine's Day. So there is a celebration already for that month."
And then she went through each month figuring which would be the best. She decided on June. Adam was thinking more around September. I was not thinking. I was holding my breath. This was a big test for my future son-in-law. Could he make her first dream come true?

The first week in July, Adam called me, breathless.

"Mom, can you keep a secret because I'm going to need your help."
Can I keep a secret! Ask any of my girlfriends. I have no memory for gossip, so when I'm told something in "great confidence," I can be depended upon. I completely forget what they told me. If they only knew.

"Mom, I'm buying the ring this week and giving it to her August 4th."
How thrilled I was! Not that he was giving her an engagement ring but that he had called me "mom." He did not see the tears in my eyes. He didn't realize much of my excitement had nothing to do with the ring.

He had it all planned. Alexandra was going to run the New York Marathon in November and August 4th there was to be a 13-mile qualifying race. After completing the 13 miles, she would go to his apartment which would be drenched with flowers and the engagement ring would be sitting in its box on the coffee table. The size and sparkle would attract her eye. I questioned whether it would be romantic to have her sweaty and drained of energy from a 13-mile run, but he thought it a perfect plan so I said, "Great!"

When August 4th arrived, my job was to get to his apartment after she started out for the run and help him arrange three hundred flowers in every receptacle in his apartment. It was fun cutting the stems and having him run around finding more "vases." It was the first time I was with him alone and I discovered how truly delightful he was. He had had *Sarabeth's* deliver Alexandra's favorite brunch, had scouted the neighborhood gathering up every available flower, and had bought a few extra vases, glass containers and sundry other 'rounds.' There were flowers in wastepaper baskets, flowers in straw beach bags, flowers in silver vases, crystal bowls, and petals floating in little dishes. His heart was beating faster than mine as we hurried to complete the scene before she returned. After a run through, with me playing Alexandra's part, he felt he could pull it off and off I went.

Two hours later my telephone rang, "Mother, Adam and I are engaged. He just gave me a ring!" she said breathlessly.
"Oh my god," I answered her screech. "Oh Ali, how wonderful," I exclaimed.

Soon they floated into my apartment. Trembling, she showed me the ring which I made believe I had not already seen.
"Oh it's magnificent, sweetheart." I said.

The next part of Adam's surprise was that he had two tickets for them to fly to Las Vegas to celebrate their engagement. He had asked me to pack her suitcase, as they had a narrow window of time to get to the airport. So, when Alexandra saw a suitcase all ready for her, she knew.

"Wow, mom, you really can keep a secret," her voice trailed out the door.

PART II

The Countdown

The Year of Your Life

After the engagement occurs and, perhaps, an engagement party, the countdown begins. You now have approximately one year to prepare for this major event. It is a year that will be the most extraordinary experience of your life.

An entire year of my existence was focused on this one evening, my daughter's wedding, and it completely took over my life even though I tried to have it otherwise. After one major decision was accomplished, there was another and another, unending decisions, follow-up and attention to detail. After finding the perfect venue where you want the wedding to take place, you go to the next item and the next and the next. For one year you live and breathe The Wedding.

When the actual countdown begins, things seem to be overwhelming. What needs to be done and what should be done first? Here is where the "lists" in bridal workbooks and magazines overwhelm. When I first saw these lists, I panicked. They looked formidable. Some went as far as outlining 18 months before the wedding when the engaged couple announced their engagement; others listed the most superfluous things just to make the lists look "important." Worst of all, many have suggestions that are truly incorrect.

In this section, I have outlined the year's preparations month-by-month and if you "chunk down" and take each month as a separate entity, you will not be overwhelmed. After the engagement is announced things begin to unfold and if you have an outline to follow, they will unfold according to a plan that takes care of first things first. The very first aspect you must discuss, which will create the parameters of the wedding, is the budget.

The Budget

When a budget is defined (even though you will probably 'stray' from the original one), you then have a foundation upon which to make decisions. Certainly, you will have a better idea of the venue you can select and the number of guests who can be invited.

The budget is often a sensitive issue because it is not discreet to discuss money. It's an uncomfortable subject. But this is one instance when you must overcome the discomfort and talk about lucre. The budget consists of many parts. There is the cost of the venue which is delineated by cost per person and is calculated according to dinner-course selections, quality and quantity of the wine, liquor and champagne, and the selections of hors d'oeuvres and the various stations that will be offered at the Reception. What is also included in the budget is the cost of all the services: the band, the florist, the musical ensemble, the photographer, and the officiant. Then there is the bridal gown and all the accoutrements for the bride and groom, presents for each member of the bridal party and miscellaneous things. The list includes:

Save-the-date cards
Invitations
An officiant
A band
A string quartet for the ceremony (optional)
A photographer
A florist
A cake maker (often included with the price per person dinner)
A wedding gown
A veil
A tiara
A mother-of-the-bride dress
Bridesmaids' dresses
Tuxedos for ushers and groom
Wedding rings
Yarmulkes
A Ketubah
Make-up artists and hair stylists for the Big Day

It certainly adds up. So it is very advisable to sit down with a list of all possible expenditures and deal with the numbers. When this is accomplished—articulated and written down!—there will never be any embarrassing moments. It is a crucial step to take. The participants in this discussion should include the bride's parents (who pay for most of the wedding) and the bride and groom. It should be the groom's place to discuss with his parents what, if anything, they would like to contribute. Traditionally, the groom's parents paid for the music and the flowers but there are no hard rules today.

6

Twelve Months Before the Wedding

Ceremony and reception:	Select a venue
Services:	Begin looking at magazines to get ideas about gowns
	Begin looking at the same magazines to explore the works of photographers
	Begin reading the blurbs in magazines about bands
	Start asking around for recommendations (friends, family, the manager at the venue, co-workers)

The first few months after the engagement is the time to **enjoy** leafing through bridal magazines and getting ideas about wedding gowns and floral arrangements and looking at the work of various photographers and obtaining the names of bands. I had folders for each category and just ripped out pictures and placed them in the various folders. They provided for a wonderful reference "library" when the actual searching began and the decisions had to be made.

But now it is twelve months before the wedding and you must find a venue. There is no relaxing until this is accomplished. On our travels through mansions and manors, we met young people who were looking to book the venue two years hence. So I am not exaggerating that one year in advance is the usual rule of thumb. That is not to say you cannot find a venue only six months in advance. It just depends upon the time of year you plan to marry and whether you have your heart set on a particular place. My friend's children easily found a venue in only four months because they were getting married in March (not a popular month because of the possibility of bad weather in the northeast). Also, they selected a botanical garden which is more popular in the spring and summer months when the flowers and fauna are dazzlingly in bloom. It was a beautiful wedding. No one commented that it was March and no one complained about the absence of flowers.

Selecting the Venue

There are a number of factors to be considered that narrow the choices and make decisions a little easier. First, it's a good idea to decide upon the season. Does the bride have her heart set on a June wedding? Or would she rather it be spring when flowers are budding and nature is blossoming? Some couples have definitive visions for their weddings. They might want an outdoor garden wedding, a church or temple wedding, a wedding ceremony on the beach, a wedding in an historical landmark building or in a wonderful Manhattan hotel.

It hardly needs to be stated that if one wants a summer wedding, one might want to look at venues where the wedding can take place out of doors. The only caveat is the weather. It can turn out to be a scorching 104 degree day or a rainy one. If the bride is a laid back young woman and can live with these uncertainties, then do it. But I have to say that many a wedding has to be taken indoors at the last minute and ends up being nothing like the one that had been planned.

Under One Roof

Another important consideration is whether to have the wedding *under one roof* or to have the ceremony in one place and the reception and dinner in another. When planning the wedding ceremony in a place of worship, albeit beautiful, several aspects must be factored in. These factors are convenience and economy of physical expenditure. To have the wedding under one roof makes it logistically easier for everyone. If the ceremony takes place in a temple of worship, after the service everyone must get into cars and drive to where the dinner and dance will be. This is not a bad idea but it does pose concerns and requires alternative plans. Again, in case of inclement weather, having the affair is one place certainly cuts down on rain-soaked clothes and hairdos. It also cuts down on losing guests en route.

Remember the suggestion to simplify. It simplifies everything to have the wedding take place at a hotel or a venue that caters weddings. First, there is a suite where the wedding party can dress so they do not have to travel from home in their gowns and tuxedoes. At a hotel, the use of the bridal suite extends all day and overnight as well which provides great leeway for the bride, the groom and the wedding party. For example, you can also arrange to have the bride's make-up and hair done in the suite which makes it easier than having her beauty needs tended to in one locale and then having to get her to the venue by some mode of transportation. Another advantage of having the wedding take place in a hotel or a wedding facility is that you do not have to deal with caterers or order liquor or attend to myriad things like having an attendant in the ladies room. Everything is taken care of by the Event Manager.

Castles in Air

I panicked when I spoke to friends because I had not known about the need to find a venue so quickly. Joyously, when I told them that Alexandra had become engaged, their congratulations were immediately followed by, "Did you get a place yet?"
"She just became engaged," I said.
They told me the scoop, "You have to reserve a place at least a year in advance."
"Oh my God," I panicked.
So while Adam and Alexandra were playing craps or whatever game they liked in Las Vegas, I was setting up appointments to see places in Westchester and New Jersey. My friend Helene squinted her eyes, pursed her lips and said warily, "I don't think castles in Westchester are for you, Sandra." At that moment I had no idea what she was talking about. I had heard of such wonderful places, stone castles, mansions, beautiful scenery and, most of all, experienced wedding planners.

The operative words are: grandeur, opulence, timeless elegance. One castle was built on a manmade hill and claimed to be the summer home of some flamboyant railroad tycoon. Another claimed to be an English country manor and had palladium-style windows and crystal chandeliers. But the castles of Italian Renaissance architecture with neo-classical interiors turned out to be ersatz, the experienced wedding planners headed up wedding factories and the beautiful scenery would be to no avail for our October wedding—but I didn't know this yet.

My daughter and my future son-in-law returned on Thursday and before they had their suitcases unpacked, I gave them the itinerary for Saturday and Sunday. Impressed with my action and agreeing that they needed to reserve a place, off we went, Leonard at the wheel.

"I don't think Westchester's the place," he warned.
He's so intuitive but I was too excited to hear him.

The first "venue" was at the tip of the peninsula off Long Island Sound that overlooked water and did have breathtaking ocean views. However, the decor of "frothy peaches and blues," beautiful on a Renoir canvas, looked tawdry on walls and threadbare chairs.
"Tacky," announced Adam.

The second place was a newly renovated conservatory complete with waterfalls, marble and gold leaf. What they didn't include in their ornate descriptive literature is that this tall, circular, all-glass building is completely surrounded by asphalt and is next to a *Mobile Gas Station*. Does the ceremony room overlook the Mobile Station I wondered, as I felt hands pulling me back to the car.
"Thank you; good-bye," I called to the wind.

Driving a little further north in Westchester we came to a large, stone mansion (they are all landmarks in Westchester!) with spectacular views of the Hudson River that boasted some connection with Mark Twain although Jacques Halle of Metropolitan banking fame replaced the house with its present stone mansion. As we entered the marble rotunda with conservatory ceiling, the woman in charge explained, "And those attending your wedding will enter a different door than the other wedding party…"
We thanked her and left.

Another castle, also overlooking the Hudson River, had a Greek hall with a 40-foot ceiling and tiffany-style glass windows. In addition, there were spears hanging on dark, dank walls and the windows had heraldic motifs—all of which seemed to suggest a backdrop for one of Henry VIII's weddings—or, better, the beheading of Anne Boleyn—rather than a modern, joyful wedding in the 21st century.

True to his usual positive self, Adam suggested we look at one more. This castle was a Greek Revival King House with a musician's balcony which meant that the dancing at the wedding would take place on an upper level. "Oh, no," thoughtful Adam said, "mum-mum could never walk up these stairs if she wanted to dance."

The next place we just looked at from the car and decided to go somewhere for lunch. I was ready for more than a lunch. A strong drink was more like it.
I felt as if I needed a course in Classical and Medieval architecture. I had seen Renaissance chapels, Tudor-style halls and castles that were supposed to be Greek-Revival. I did not want a king's ransom; all I wanted was a tasteful wedding venue.

"Let's cancel tomorrow," we chimed in unison.
If Westchester wasn't for us, then New Jersey wedding factories furnished in glitzy Renaissance Royale would certainly depress us even more.

My mission, then, was to find a place in Manhattan—one that was both tasteful and under a hundred grand. A mission not too impossible, I thought, since the number in our wedding party would be comparatively small. My family consisted of two sisters, their husbands, a niece and her husband and a nephew with the present woman in his life. I knew I could probably unearth a cousin or two but that was all.

There are magazines and Websites filled with wedding venues, from lofts in Soho to the famed *Plaza Hotel* to the *Botanical Gardens*, in Brooklyn or the Bronx. My first appointment was at the *The Plaza* because it was on Central Park South and Alexandra had requested being near Central Park for picture-taking. She had relinquished her desire for a summer wedding when I reminded her how muggy summers are in New York City. Also, I reminded her that she disliked the tendrils that suddenly encircle her face when the humidity rose. September is filled Jewish holidays, as is early October, so we decided on October 18th—until we found out it, too, was a Jewish holiday. So now we were at the end of October trying to figure out if there would still be leaves on the trees at that time.

At the *Plaza*, the manager took me perfunctorily through the routine. In the brochure that he handed me was an article about a wedding of a famous person that had taken place at the hotel. The accompanying picture displayed a dazzlement of candles and tinsel that made the space look like St. Petersburg after a tremendous snowstorm. I knew his ennui was me. I was not a famous star from Tinsel Town.

"Is this the chair covering?" I asked, feeling the rough muslin overthrow between my fingers.

"Oh, if you want damask that's extra."

"And the silverware?" I queried about the silver-plated spoons and forks and knives.

"Oh if you want the ones with the Plaza signature, that's extra," he said unblinkingly.

He explained that the ceremony would take place on the first floor in the *Rose Room* and the dinner and dancing would take place in the second floor *Terrace Room*.

"You mean, the wedding party will have to walk through the lobby, pass the Palm Court and walk up the stairs?" I wondered aloud.

"Yes," he answered.

"Thank you. Goodbye."

The event manager at another well-known Central Park South hotel snapped, "You need a minimum of 225 people."
"Thank you. Goodbye."

My next appointment took me to a loft in Tribeca. It looked gorgeous and huge in the glossy magazine and boasted a 360 degree view of the city from Wall Street to Times Square. What the magazine didn't reveal was the Otis elevator the guests would have to ride in order to reach the top floor. The room was lovely but a little bare and the restrooms were public toilets.
"Thank you. Goodbye."

When Tim, the caterer I had used for the engagement party, called me to thank me for the referral I had sent, I pounced on him.
"Tim, perhaps you can help. I need a place for the wedding."
Delighted, he proceeded to show me a lovely embassy on Park Avenue that had beautiful marble pillars and a sweeping staircase that led to a smallish, unattractive room where the wedding would take place. Next he took me to an Old World museum on Central Park West ("Do they keep the pictures on the walls," I was amazed) that required rentals from the dance floor to the napkins.
"Thank you. Goodbye."

Exhausted and pressured for time, I thought about my own neighborhood and walked into a few hotels nearby. One, known for its power breakfasts, had a beautiful mirrored ceiling and a cramped antechamber where the cocktail hour would take place.

The Catering Manager at another beautiful hotel showed us an unmirrored Versailles Suite and a postage-size dance floor. The floor plan revealed a suite that was 1,300 square feet.
"It's a closet," I marveled, thinking of my apartment almost twice the size.
"We're redoing the space. I've been telling them for years the dance floor isn't large enough," said the hostess.
"When will it be completed?" I politely asked.
"Oh, I'm sure it will be in time for your wedding," she muttered.
"Thank you. Good-bye."

Next was the *Pierre* with its neoclassic spire and distinctive copper roof (that's what the literature said). Who sees the roof, I wondered. But I wanted to see what they claimed was the "undisputed choice." The *Grand Ballroom*, an over-garlanded, tromp l'oeil garden, seemingly in its original 1930s state, rivals the Frick's *Fragonard Room*.

It is 8,500 ostentatious square feet and can accommodate 750 guests.
"Breathless," I said, for want of uttering anything nearer the truth.
The event manager explained, "We don't have various selections for the dinner or optional stations at the cocktail hour. It's the same for everyone. We charge a flat $450 per person."
"Thank you. Goodbye."

At the other end of the spectrum was a very modern hotel, very *dernier cri*, and as minimal as its name. Modern, clean décor with natural wood floors and earth tones was a little too minimal for me. Their "perfect marriage of natural serenity and modern design" is good for meditation but not a festive wedding. A young woman showed us the various rooms: *The Forest Room*, the *Waterfall Room*, the *Sea Room* and the *Earth Room*.
"Where is the Sleep Room?" I asked sleepily.
"Thank you. Good-bye."

It was only August. Alexandra and Adam were getting married 14 months hence, but I was getting nervous. I was running out of ideas. I had looked at many hotels and lofts and didn't know where else to go in Manhattan.

Then I strolled up Madison Avenue and came upon a small, lovely boutique hotel nestled on 77th Street, quiet and elegant, exactly as its architect, Sir John Soame, had envisioned. There was no pretension of being a castle, no tiffany-style, no trompe l'oeil designs, no ersatz copy of anything! It was not cavernous nor was it claustrophobic. Like Goldilocks, I had found the perfect place for Alexandra and Adam's wedding. Not too soft nor too lumpy—but just right.

Discreetly accented with 18th century Piranesi prints and Biedermeier furniture, *The Mark Hotel* boasts a 5 star restaurant in its characteristically quiet way. The Events Manager took me to the Townhouse floor to show me the space. It was simple and tasteful. The décor, pale mauve and beige with damask linen and matching chair covers (at no extra cost!), bone porcelain china and pale, persimmon carpeting throughout was perfect. It just connected with me and I felt content. And that's the secret to finding the venue for your daughter's wedding. It has to be who you are—what your lifestyle is.

The Mark Hotel was for me—sedate and tasteful—but was it for Alexandra and Adam? Nervously, I showed them the entrance lobby. I took them up the small marble Italianate winding staircase to the Townhouse floor.

"To the left are *The Greenhouse* and the *Drawing Room* where the cocktail hour can take place," explained our charming guide, Alessandro. "To the right are *Mark I* and *Mark II* and *Mark III*, three rooms that sweep into one when the walls are receded."

"This is where the ceremony will take place," I stretched my hand across the expanse.

"It's a long aisle to walk," Alexandra noted, with relish.

They loved it. They loved the flow, the simplicity, the Piranesi prints, the china, the silverware, the brocade linen, the location (a step from Central Park).

"We'll take it," we told Alessandro, in unison.

Whew! We had the place where the wedding would occur. Now I thought I could relax. Except that now came all the rest—the searching, the comparing, the listening, the researching, the decision-making, the challenges, the mistakes, the wasting of time, the joy, the pain, the elation, the fatigue, the happiness and the stress-filled days. I returned to my list of all that remained to be done.

Which should be tackled first, I wondered.

I had twelve months to get this wedding together and wondered where to begin. Having all this time for preparation was both a luxury and a torture. A luxury because I didn't feel pressured for time and a torture because there was too much time which made for drawn-out, belaboring decisions.

7

Losing a Daughter

At about this time in the process, it hits you that a major change is occurring in your life. A wonderful person who has been an integral part of your every day and who has been unconditionally yours has now become part yours and part some-one else's. And this wonderful person is now going to share her life with someone other than you. She will go on trips—with someone else. She will go to the the-atre—with someone else. She will share her innermost thoughts—with another person. You suddenly come head on with the painful fact that you are losing your daughter. And it crashes on you like a tsunami.

"Mom, Adam and I are going to Iceland for four or five days," Alexandra announced.
"So far?" was all I could utter.
"But mom," Alexandra explained, "it's so close; it's a four hour plane ride."
And of course she had done her research and knew every crater to see, where to go horseback riding, every lava field, icecap, hotspring and geyser. She knew the best hotel in Reykjavik and the restaurants as well. They went swimming in the Lan-gardalur outdoor pool and the man-made beach with heated sea water. They took a trip to the Blue Lagoon, a spa located near Grindavik and had massages and mud packs. Their description of Iceland was so exhilarating that it lured Barbara and Barry to go there soon after.
"It's only four hours away," became a humorous catch-phrase in our lives.
"What a delight, my daughter is," I thought to myself.

"Lucky Adam," I mentioned to Leonard.
"He doesn't know how lucky he is," Leonard complained. He was becoming grumpy lately. I guess he knew before I did.

Then she sprang it.

"Mother, you said when Adam and I were engaged, then I could live with him. Well, we're engaged now."
What could I say? Wait a little longer? Stay here with me and just spend weekends at his place? I was supposed to be the thoroughly modern mother.

Alexandra and I had been so close for so many years. Truly, she was my best friend. We went to the movies together; we saw the ballet together; we went to the theatre all the time. I have saved all the love letters she wrote to me from summer camp. I have saved all the passionate letters she wrote to me from college—filled with her feelings, her experiences, her doubts, her troubles. We spent two weeks together in London, when she studied abroad in her senior year in college, traipsing through Piccadilly, sighing over the Turners at the *Tate*, seeing the musical "Martin Guerre" twice because she loved it so, driving up to Stratford-on-Avon to see the Bard's home and thrilling to an incomparable "Henry V" staged with no scenery and men wearing horse's costumes.

We were not mother and daughter—we were best friends. There was never a man between us—no father, no boyfriend. Now there was a fiancé.

Leonard consoled me, "I'm here now, sweetheart." And perhaps that was a strong deciding factor. Why should she live with Leonard and me and not with her fiancé? So off she went. It helped that it was only 16 blocks north of where I lived—even on the same side of town. It also helped that my delicious almost son-in-law would call and say, "Hi mom," and ended our conversations with, "I love you." I told myself that I was not losing a daughter but gaining another son and it was consoling to me that Alexandra had this special person in her life and no longer had to depend solely on me.

There's a wonderful opening to one of Ann Tyler's novels where an elderly mother is on her deathbed and is saying to one of her sons who had always wanted more from her than she was able to give, "You should have had another." When he questions what the "another" is referring to, she responds, "Another mother." I had strongly identified with this, my being a single mother bringing up two children. I felt that there was not enough of me and certainly I couldn't be both father and mother. If they didn't have a father, it would have been nice for all of us if they could have had two mothers. But now something even better was happening to Alexandra. She had a fiancé and was marrying a young man who would be her best friend, her confidante, her lover.

But when she actually took her things and moved to Adam's apartment, something happened to my heart. Even though she was 16 blocks from me, I missed her. Even though I was thrilled for her, I missed her. A little bright light had gone out in the house—not to see her beautiful face at the end of each day, not to hear her cheerful voice (even if it was speaking to her friends on the telephone), not to hear her laughter, in the next room, when she watched some silly sitcom. There was an emptiness that all the loving from Leonard could not fill. My little girl was gone forever.

It has nothing to do with the cliché "empty nest syndrome." I was not in a long-term marriage and suddenly finding myself alone with a husband of 35 or 40 years, with little to say to him. I was in a vibrant, rather new relationship that was exciting and filled my days. I didn't feel empty. I missed Alexandra, the present-day Alexandra. I wasn't missing the baby, the little girl. I wasn't reminiscing, remembering her first steps or her performance in a school play. That was the past and I didn't yearn for it. I wanted Alexandra as she was now. I wanted my dearest, most trusted friend to come back and live with me.

I thought of what I had said often in my life—about bringing children up to be independent and to lead their own lives. It sounded so "modern" and so damn "civilized." Well, at this point in my life I didn't feel like being the Modern Mother.
I cried; I wailed. I wanted my daughter back.

"But mom, I live right near you. And anyway; you haven't lost a daughter. You're gaining another son."
"Oh, yeah. I'd be gaining another son if you and Adam came to live with me!" I cried.
And don't think I hadn't fantasized this happening.
I told Leonard, "They could make the den into a bedroom. They'd have the terrace and their own bathroom."
He didn't think it was a bad idea, either. I realized he missed her, too. Although she is not his biological daughter, he thinks she is and he loves her deeply.

8

Ten Months Before the Wedding

Services: Interview bands, listen to their CDs and contract with
                             one
                             Interview trios or quartets (for the ceremony) and con-
                             tract with one

Musical Strains: Contracting With Bands and String Quartets

Ten months before the wedding is a good time to begin to interview bands and string quartets and trios (optional). Yes, you have plenty of time. But the closer you get to the wedding the more stress you are going to feel so I advise you to get as much as possible accomplished when there seems to be "all the time in the world."

When it comes to bands, I strongly suggest recommendations. There are so many bands and, I am sure, most are good. Thus, to simplify the process of investigating dozens of bands, narrowing it down to a few recommendations is a good idea. Since you cannot attend an actual wedding to hear them play, you have to go to their studio or listen to a CD or watch a video of them performing. I found the experience of going to their studio to be least successful because it's so artificial. They get a few of their group together for the "audition" and play and sing, but it's unadorned and, somehow, it doesn't work. I think it cannot show them off at their best. CDs are chancy because you don't know what the performers look like and you cannot be sure the same players will appear at your wedding. So videos are probably the best. It shows the band at its best—playing at an actual wedding.

You must make sure the players with whom you contract will be the same who show up the night of the wedding. However, since you contract often a year or at least six months before the wedding, people can drop out and new faces can appear. Just make sure this aspect is discussed. The band should be a group whose members are used to playing together and not one where the leader hires out different musicians for every gig.

Define everything very clearly right from the beginning. Ask how they take their "breaks" and insist on continuous music, if that's what you want, with one or two players taking a break while the remainder of the band continues to play. Of course, the bigger the band, the less obvious their breaks will appear. We had an eight-piece band that included: keyboard, guitar, drums, 3 horns and 2 lead vocalists.

Because of aesthetics, you might consider asking that they not have the name of their band "advertised" in front of them. It is the one detail I did not think about and, thus, in every picture where someone came to the front of the dance floor, the band's placard appears in the background. So when I gave my welcoming speech and when Barry said the blessing on the wine and Leonard blessed the *challah*, there is their placard, like a billboard on the side of a road. I suggest asking them for business cards and promising to hand them out or leave them on the reception table.

The most important aspect is to meet and talk to the lead person in the band. This way, you can discuss the type of music you want played, you can communicate the "tone" of the wedding that you want them to create, and you can establish a rapport with him or her that will pay off tremendously the night of the wedding.

Since you will most probably hire the band about ten months before the wedding, it is imperative that you draw up a contract, so there can be no misunderstandings two weeks or two days before the wedding.

PUT IT ALL IN WRITING.
At the time you hire the band, you will probably be asked to make a deposit of 50% of the total cost which is anywhere from $8,000 to $20,000. When putting that much money down, everything must be in writing.

The contract should contain the following:

What time they will arrive

What equipment, if any, they will need

The names of each player

How they will take their breaks

When they will eat dinner

What types of music they will play (three weeks before the wedding you should meet with the bandleader and enumerate specific numbers you want them to play)

Their cancellation policy

What they will wear (one requirement might be no earrings in the men's ears)

Music, From Dionysian to Sacral

There are different musical requirements for the two very distinct segments of the wedding. One is the ceremony and the other is the dinner/dance. One is the solemn and beautiful *sacre*, the religious rites; the other is the secular, the Dionysian drinking, dining and dancing. Although the ceremonial music was of greater importance to me, it was more urgent to obtain a band first. Everyone hires a band; not everyone has a string quartet for the ceremony.
So our immediate challenge was to hire a band.

"Mother, Adam and I know nothing about music. I'm leaving the band up to you," Alexandra declared one day. What did I know? Dancing to Tito Puente at *El Patio Beach Club*, in Long Beach, when I was 19, didn't make me a dance maven. Moreover, since my *cha cha* days, all I have listened to has been classical music. I knew I needed help so I gathered a band committee. Leonard loves to dance and, certainly, I thought, would know a good dance band when he heard one. My son, much to my dismay, knows the music of the day; he even knows the lyrics.

So the three of us began to interview bands. Armed with a list of names of bands gathered from magazines and recommendations from *The Mark* and from friends, the interviews began.

One band consisted of a group of kids who thought wedding music should be loud and full of them singing and entertaining (what they thought was entertaining). They laughed and *kibitzed* and seemed to get a kick out of themselves. Stop the music!!! Another group was represented by a woman who, dressed in a *mou mou* and whose aptronym should have been Mrs. Scatterbrain, rummaged through a stack of material on a desk that rivaled the Collier brothers. Finally, she found a few pages of music that the band played and then surprised herself by locating a CD. Thanks but no thanks. Many are good bands but their lead singers are performers manqué—thinking they are reincarnations of Frank Sinatra or Vic Damone. Dreadlocks, earrings in noses, jumping from the stage to the dance floor were out of the question as far as I was concerned.

We interviewed bands four nights in a row—in live studios, listening to CDs, watching videos. We were beginning to argue among ourselves—not a good sign. At our last appointment, we were greeted by a woman, a pleasant, normal-looking adult woman dressed in a business suit. No kimonos or miniskirts, no flaming red or shoe polish black hair, no messy office and no sales pitch. She spoke quietly, albeit slightly imperiously, but I felt she had an excellent command of the business (not just the music). She knew *The Mark* and their bands had played there often. We were seated in a well-appointed office on a leather sofa and we watched the video of their three bands.

She sized me up and I think she knew before I had decided which band I would select. It wasn't the one her son led which was too electronic for me. It wasn't even the one which her husband lead; his band had too much of a "big band" sound and I wanted more than Glen Miller at Alexandra and Adam's wedding. She seemed to know that I wanted a group that had excellent soloists but who, instead of being filled with themselves, were filled with talent and the ability to give of themselves to their audience.

She knew the group I wanted. The lead player, a superb guitarist, would also be the emcee. He had a good voice and diction, he was warm yet professional and I knew he'd say nothing extraneous. Jason had warned me, "Mom, we better not get anyone who's going to make announcements about Uncle Brucey…" I knew what he meant. He wanted a simple, "Ladies and gentlemen let us welcome the bride and groom for their first dance." Period, end of sentence. No corny comments, no commentary at all.

We took the band.

The committee immediately dissolved when it came to selecting a string quartet. That was my realm and only mine. The choices are fewer than those of bands and it is easier to discern their talent by inquiring about their musical studies and listening to them play. After calling several groups and speaking with their lead player, I connected with Allegra. When she told me she was the Musical Director at the *Marlboro Summer Music Festival,* in Vermont, I knew I had found a gem. When I listened to their CD, I knew the gem was a rare one. When she came to my home and discussed ideas with me, the gem became priceless. So now that we had the quartet, selecting the appropriate music was the challenge for me.

The melodies that waft through the air during the ceremony guiding each member of the wedding party as he or she walks down the aisle sets the mood so I wanted the music to be carefully selected. For me, this translated into hours and hours of listening and re-listening to my favorite composers. Of course, many were far from appropriate for a wedding and much was too familiar. No *Air on a G String* for my daughter, nor Mendelssohn's *Wedding March*. Sibelius was too slow and Mahler too morose. Handel was too common and Vivaldi, wonderful Vivaldi, who is now wait time music on the telephone, could not be a contender. I loved Tchaikovsky's *Theme* from *Romeo and Juliet*, the first movement of Bizet's *Symphony in C* (would people recognize the theme from the Pianos, Pianos advertisement on FM 96.3?), Liszt's *Nocturne #3 in A Flat Major* (could it be transcribed for strings?) the second movement of Beethoven's *Piano Concerto #5* (could it be played a little faster?), Hayden's *Serenade* (bravo! it's for a string quartet) to name a few. There were Bach's *Brandenburg Concerto #1 in F*, the first movement, Handel's *Water Music*, *Anitra's Dance* from *Peer Gynt*, Suite #1, opus 46, and the allegro from Tchaikovsky's *Capriccio Italien*.

But above all, for the bride's walk down the aisle, I loved Massenet's *Meditation* from *Thais*. Another strong contender for her walk down the aisle was the *Intermezzo* from Mascagni's *Cavalieri Rusticana*.

About the time I was focused on the ceremony music, the Hoffman family came into the city for brunch. I thought a wonderful after-brunch activity would be for everyone to come to my home and listen to the various possibilities. Everyone agreed it was a grand idea, except my daughter. Knowing my strong feelings about music, she had her hesitations.

I, however, was thrilled. I had a captive audience and began my presentation. As I played each selection, it was all too obvious which I favored; this, of course, made it difficult for anyone to truly voice his or her opinion. When someone suggested Vivaldi's *Spring*, I responded too emphatically, "Oh, too common." With my flare for drama, I hushed everyone to listen carefully.
"What's that piece?" someone queried.
"*Barcarolle* from *Tales of Hoffman*," I sang in response to this seemingly improbable question.
Alexandra shot a warning glance at me.
"What about Pachobel?" someone else suggested.
"Too funereal," I shot back instantly.

Silence. I was losing my audience. Quickly, I went for my coup. I wanted so much to translate my vision of Alexandra walking down the aisle to the plaintive, ephemeral notes, so Alexandra could feel what I felt and envision what I saw. With hope pressing hard in my heart, I played the *Meditation* from *Thais* and was crushed when my daughter said, "I can't picture myself walking down the aisle to that."

Adam, much less picayune than his bride, simply requested a march-tempo and strongly in the running was Clarke's *Trumpet Voluntary* or Purcell's *Trumpet Tune in D*. Barry begged that the music not elicit the feeling of birds chirping; ergo, no harp. Otherwise, he had no definite selection in mind. I had little interference when it came to the bridesmaids, as *Salut D'Amour* was perfect accompaniment for beautiful, long-haired, long-frocked young ladies. Also, none was present at this afternoon gathering. As my audience either remained quiet or resisted my selections, I became more vocal in what I preferred.

Later that evening, alone with my daughter, she explained why little had been accomplished.
"Mother you were so strong in your opinions."
"Well," I harrumphed, "if people disagreed, they could have spoken up."
I suppose it's not that easy to disagree with me when I am rapturous.

Tactfully, my daughter suggested that I call the leader of the ensemble we had selected and get her advice. I contacted Allegra! The emails flew across the Web. Allegra, far off in Vermont involved with the Marlboro Music Festival, responded to my lame queries with the attention that a Queen's coronation might warrant. She, too, rhapsodized over the *Intermezzo*. The *Meditation* from *Thais,* she explained, placed too much emphasis on the violinist which would detract from the bride. I had Allegra's vote!

Alexandra still wasn't convinced but since it was only July, I knew I had a few months to negotiate.

9

Eight Months Before the Wedding

Finding the Perfect Wedding Dress

Gown: Order wedding gown

That's it—just one thing to do! There is only one major thing you need to do eight months before the wedding—select a wedding gown. However, I cannot misrepresent. Although it is only one item, it is not an easy task. One major reason it is so stressful is that the anxious bride has not been given good advice. In truth, if done correctly, it should be a delightful experience.

First, the tense bride feels pressured for time. She has heard horror stories about gowns not being ready on time. However, even though bridal salons say they need eight months, I know young women who have decided they were getting married just five or six months before their wedding date and somehow they had gowns and didn't walk down the aisle naked. So, don't panic.

Mostly it is the hype that makes the search for the perfect wedding dress so formidable. One popular wedding site has 138 designers listed and you can spend days (their site is very slow!) calling up each designer and getting several pictures of their wedding gowns. However, I found that of the 138 designers, I was interested in only 2; the remainder were unknown names and the better known couture designers were blatantly missing. So, enough for sites.

A good beginning is to peruse bridal magazines and pull out the pictures of those gowns that appeal to you the most. You might want to make a first stop at a department store Bridal Salon as they have several designers represented. This is your exploratory stage. Take notes on what you like—color, style, etc. Then you might want to visit a few salons and continue trying on various dresses. At this point, you will probably be able to narrow things down. You'll know if you want a very large skirt or a drop waist. You might also be able at this stage to decide that you want a strapless or a scoop or long sleeves.

Again, the sites seem to be filled with an abundance of advice but much of it is superfluous. They seem to assume a woman has never bought a dress before. I think women know what looks best on them. For example, if you are full-busted I think you know that a *halter top* is not going to be flattering; if you are full-waisted I think you already know that an *A-line* gown is not the best for your figure. Just go with the knowledge you have accumulated for the past 20 + years of shopping for dresses.

There area a few basics that we might review here:
The *Cinderella* has a fitted bodice and a bell-shaped skirt. It hides a lot below the waist!
The *Empire* has a high feminine waist and if you have a "full" midriff, this style hides it!
The *A-line* or *Princess* requires a small waist and a flat stomach, but it hides a large derriere and thighs.
The *sheath* closely follows the line of the body and, as far as I am concerned, doesn't belong on a bride. A bride should look beautiful and virginal.
There are a number of *corset*-style bodices that hold in the midriff nicely but you have to like the look of boning and lace-ups.
The V-shape of a *Basque waist* is very flattering and is usually on a full bell-shaped skirt.
The *mermaid* look is best for fish and, again, is too slinky for a bride

After you try on the various silhouettes, you'll see what looks good on you.

Then, you will want to decide on a neckline. There's the bateau, the jewel, round, square, sweetheart, V-neck, scoop, strapless, spaghetti strap and mandarin. Again, it depends upon your bust.

Access you body:
Are you short-waisted? Try a princess
Are you thick-waisted? Try the Empire.

Are you full-figured? A ball gown hides a great deal.
Are you pear-shaped? A strapless or a Basque waist is flattering.
Are you thin? Anything will look good on you!
Are you petite? Don't overwhelm with a ballgown but almost anything will look good.

There are also myriad **fabrics** that you might want to be familiar with. Some are:
Chiffon—delicate and sheer, made from silk or rayon
Crepe—thin material with a crinkled surface
Damask—similar to brocade, but lighter, with raised design
Duchesse—lightweight hybrid of silk and rayon woven into a satin finish
Faille—a structured ribbed finish, usually firm
Organdy—stiff and transparent fabric
Organza—crisp and sheer like chiffon, but with a stiffer texture
Peau de Soie—soft, satin-faced high quality cloth with a dull luster and a grainy appearance
Satin—a heavy, smooth fabric with a high sheen
Silk—a soft fabric noted for its elasticity
Shantung—similar to raw silk which has a rough, knobbed texture

Cinderella Pouf

"Nine thousand dollars for 5 hours," my daughter screeched, in disbelief, her eyes wide and her voice two octaves higher than middle C.
"I refuse, mother," she stated and I saw her mind clamping shut.
Her high decimal-level locution was in response to a wedding dress I had seen at a Madison Avenue boutique.

We're going to *Kleinfeld's*," she announced.
"Brooklyn?" I moaned.
"Brooklyn?" Leonard moaned, in resigned repetition. It was Alexandra's wish and he would never refuse what she wanted. He hired a car and off we went to the largest wedding-gown factory/salon in, it seems, all the world. Hundreds of white gowns sheathed in plastic hang from rack upon rack in several rooms. There were girls there from North Carolina and one had flown in from California; we were told they even come from England. After a few minutes, neither Leonard nor I could figure out why—why young women would get on planes to come here to buy their gowns. "Maybe where they live there are no bridal salons," Alexandra said. Intent on proving us wrong in our assessment, she found two dresses to try on. One looked a little interesting in that the Cinderella skirt, a large pouf skirt, also had some tucks throughout but when she looked into the mirror, she exclaimed, "I feel like a lampshade." Off with the gown! The second was a strapless lace gown with a large satin sash that trailed down the back. All I could say was, "This lampshade looks too Victorian."

Leonard shook his head from side to side. "Come on, sweetheart, let's go back to the city."

Then we made the rounds: Michelle Roth, Amsale, Vera Wang, Reem Acra and many more. We were shown ivory gowns, white gowns, champagne colored gowns; gowns with bodices flecked with crystals, ensconced with pearls; drop waists, puffed out skirts, slim skirts.

"I feel like a dowager queen," said Alexandra when she came out of one dressing room dragging ten yards of satin and pulling up a crystal-encrusted bodice that was more like a breastplate. "How does one dance in this?" she asked.
"Never mind dancing. How are you going to walk down the aisle?" I added.

The spectrum runs the gamut from skimpy negligees to ball gowns befitting Marie Antoinette. There are slithery sheaths, seemingly nightgowns; strapless, halter top, square-necked; sleeveless, cap sleeves, long sleeves; long trains, no trains, bustles; duchess satin, grosgrain, organza overlays.

The choices were overwhelming. There was a soft organza sheath, a strapless with shirred bodice that descended into a ladylike skirt blooming with appliquéd flowers. There was a sleeveless silk taffeta featuring a scooped neckline with a ruched and buttoned bodice and full ball skirt. There was a two-piece Dulcianna satin and French tulle ensemble with an asymmetrical drape and semi-cathedral train. Some gowns had beadwork and embroidery seemingly inspired by the Medieval Period; others were thick with Venise or Guipare lace. There were skirts that were architectural and some that were fantastically layered.

When she stepped out of one fitting room—in a nightgown! the designer pointed out that it was "feminine yet tailored, minimal yet engineered."
Were we buying a wedding dress or a design for a new home?
As if he were a time traveler, one designer stated that his gowns had "a modern sophisticated look that takes you back in time." Huh?

Several designers promised Alexandra she'd look like Audrey Hepburn or Grace Kelly.
"Who is Grace Kelly, mom?" Alexandra turned to me.
"Not important," I said and whisked her out the door.
When one rhapsodized that the fabric "speaks to me and tells me what it wants to do," we ran.
We became terrified by the tasteless choices.
Sales women were more practical than designers. They attempted to help with the query, "What image do you want to present?"
"Not Little Bo-Peep," responded Alexandra to the lace-frilled extravaganza that the sales woman was showing her.
Others offered the cliché, "You'll know when you see it."
I encouraged with "oohs" and "it's beautiful" for every gown she donned—thus, I was of little help. Alexandra, more discerning, pointed out every shortcoming of each gown she tried on.

On the third Saturday of wedding dress shopping, as I sat in the Bridal Department of Saks Fifth Avenue, a vision of beauty came into view and tears smarted my eyes.

The salesperson announced, "This is it! When the mother cries, that's the dress for the bride."

"My mother cries over everything," Alexandra informed the saleswoman, but she, too, seemed to like what presented in the mirror. It was champagne and perhaps, we pondered, the color didn't make it look so bridal and that's what we liked. The one hesitation Alexandra had was that the skirt ballooned out from the waist. When she smoothed her hands down the sides of the bodice, she knew, "Oh mother, I definitely want Duchesse satin." So, it was the material that she loved.

That it was a trunk show killed the deal for Alexandra. She certainly was not ready to commit to this dress, this very day—and tomorrow the dresses would be off to another city and another trunk show. Our quest for the perfect wedding gown had not ended.

Saturday followed Saturday until it was cutting it close—or so the sales people warned us. "We need eight months from the time of ordering to delivery," haunted us and we were now into the middle of February. That gave us eight months!

"Marco Polo needed less time to bring silks back from the Orient," I quipped.

At the next couture, we discovered that Alexandra looked best in a dropped waist, which emphasizes the bride's small waist. But the skirt can billow out of a dropped waist which Alexandra named "Cinderella poofy." When the sales woman suggested taking a bodice from one dress and putting it on the skirt of another, my daughter gave me the high sign.

"Mommy, why do I have to imagine a gown? We have four more places left to see."

I had no idea there were so many bridal houses on this one small island of Manhattan. But we were running out of Saturdays.

My peripatetic mate likes to take walks, sometimes to buy a sweet and sometimes to smoke a cigar. This particular night, knowing how desperate the wedding gown situation was getting, he decided to walk up Madison Avenue.

Upon his arrival home, he announced, "I found the perfect wedding gown for Ali." From any other man, such a proclamation might warrant a smile and a pat on the cheek—but not from Leonard. He has an excellent eye for woman's clothing and knows just what looks best on whom. Wasn't it he who walked into *Bloomingdale's* and found the most smashing dress for Alexandra to wear to her Engagement Party? While we were scurrying around, looking through racks of dresses, he went to the fourth floor, saw a black boucle knit dress on a mannequin and knew it was perfect for Alexandra's curvaceous figure. "This is the most beautiful dress I have ever had in my life," she had exclaimed.

So when he returned from his evening meandering and pronounced that he had found the wedding dress for Ali, I took him very seriously. He had seen it in the window—well, not exactly; it was a picture of a gown in the front piece of the store window. As I stood beside him on 75th and Madison Avenue, I asked, "How can you tell from a picture?"
"Trust me," was all he said.

That Saturday, we were "doing" Madison Avenue again—a famous Japanese bridal couture, a famous Spanish designer and a comparatively unknown bridal salon, *Clea Colet*. In the first salon, my daughter's beautiful bosom fought the confines of gowns made for girls in puberty. At the second salon, there was not even one dress she wanted to try on.

We walked out of the store and my daughter began to cry. Can you imagine what a mother feels when her tall, beautiful, graceful daughter, after a month of shopping more than 15 bridal salons, has not found a gown for her wedding day? My heart constricted. How could this be happening—to my daughter? Why couldn't we find the perfect wedding dress? I started crying, too.

There it was—the impotency, the helplessness as I stood there and watched my child cry. I couldn't simply say, "Don't cry, sweetheart. Everything will be all right." Everything was wrong! She was getting married in *The Mark Hotel* to the dancing strains of the MS band—in the nude! Where were we going to find a wedding gown?

Leonard put his arm around her waist, kissed her on the cheek and told her, "Come on, sweetheart, your gown is waiting for you."

We walked up the stairs, entered the usual looking bridal salon with soft, cushy chairs and plush carpeting where Inga began her presentation. Her eyes swept from Alexandra's crown to toe and she said with sanguine assurance, "You probably want a strapless to show off your bodice, a dropped waist to accentuate yours and something simple yet elegant with a train and satin buttons running down the back. Perhaps Duchess satin with a touch of lace and for your fair skin I would suggest ivory, not white."

That was it. She had just described the dress Alexandra was seeking but had not yet seen. Inga pushed aside the balloon-skirted dresses, the ornamented ones with baubles, the ones that had lace form bodice to hem, the slinky ones that looked like night gowns and brought out—well, you know, the one Leonard had selected from the picture.

When Alexandra walked towards us in the dress, we began to cry. She truly looked like a Princess, in a satin strapless gown that came in at the waist and gently sloped down to the floor. Lace circled the bottom of the dress and extended along the length of the train and satin buttons glided down the back. And that was the dress. Simple and elegant like Sargent's "Madame X."

"I feel like a Princess," she softly whispered as she stood motionless in front of the mirror, entranced with the vision reflected in it.

10

Six Months Before the Wedding

Services: Interview various florists and discuss floral arrangements
Interview photographers and see samples of their work

You have half a year before the wedding. Still plenty of time; still time to enjoy all the planning. At this point, it is a good idea to seek out a florist and a photographer. Remember those folders you created with pictures ripped out of magazines? They are filled with some beautiful ideas. Also, remember your Event Manager at the venue; he or she has tremendous experience, so ask for recommendations.

Your next step is to interview. Remember the magic number—three. Interview three florists. Interview three photographers. Listen to what they have to say about their craft. For example, listen to the florist's suggestions about appropriate flowers for the time of year of your wedding. See if he or she is open to your ideas. Make sure you can work with the person. Ask the photographers to see samples of their work. Make sure you and the photographer really communicate. The personality of the photographer is very important because you are going to spend a full day and evening with him or her. So you need really to get along! When you have made your decisions, write up contracts.

A Rose is a....Cymbidium

The red rose whispers of passion, and the white rose breathes of love.-John Boyle O'Reilly

I love roses.

"I must carry cymbidiums," Alexandra stated emphatically, "that's the first flower Adam gave to me."

I had never heard of cymbidiums and they didn't sound very beautiful to me.

"But roses are so perfect for a bride," I almost pleaded. "How about roses mixed with white ranunculi?"

"What about calla lilies?" Alexandra wondered.

"With long green stalks against your wedding gown?"

"How about ruffled cattleya orchids?" I asked.

"Ruffles? For me, mother?" Alexandra complained.

We were definitely not on the same page.

Since Alexandra was the artistic one, I decided to give her this job.

"You will select the flowers!" I announced.

And with that, I had one less item on my list.

Alexandra is the family artist who designed ceramic vases that I display among my *Baccarat.* She can cook vegetables and display them so artfully on a simple glass plate while I, on the other hand, have to enhance my offerings with elaborate silver trays. I trusted Alexandra's aesthetic sensibilities and knew she would select soft colors—if not all white—for her wedding bouquet.

It was the centerpieces that I wanted to research. Color—bold color against the pale beige and pink of *The Mark.* Purple anemonies, plum scabiosa, purple sweetpeas, blue delphinium, lavender mini-calla lilies, magenta dahlias. Burgundy—that was it. Burgundy hydrangea or orchids with soft chartreuse lady's mantle or burgundy amaranthus. Mango—mango calla lilies, mango congo roses, mango tulips! Burgundy, chocolate, mango—these, I thought, were fabulous fall colors.

And, coincidentally, wherever I looked, I saw cymbidiums.

"Ali," I left a message on her tape, "cymbidiums are gorgeous. We must include them."

She must have really appreciated that!

There were cymbidiums in every color—green, white, pastel, mango. And they blended so beautifully with roses and calla lilies.

Tulips were out—not the season and they wilted so quickly. Lilies as lovely as they look have a strong aroma that often is not pleasing. But we did seem to like those funny ranunculi.

"What's stephanotis?" I wondered.

"They look like formal daisies," Alexandra explained.

"Cymbidium orchids paired with wildcat orchid in golden tallow and chocolate mini calla lilies," I suggested.

"Um, sounds luscious," Alexandra responded.

The more we researched, the more we realized that all the florists had more or less the same suggestions. All suggested appropriate flowers according to the season. Berries are often suggested for fall—berzelia berries, hypericum berries, etc. And all have various ties—velvet ribbon and pearl pins, ties made of ribbon and ties of equisidium.

Alexandra decided to select the florist with whom she had the best rapport. Marilyn of *Belle Fleur* was her selection. And what a wise decision. She is not only an experienced floral arranger but also an experienced woman who knows how to listen and when to suggest.

"Yes, I think it's a wonderful concept to have centerpieces that are dramatic and made up of darker colors. It will complement the décor of *The Mark*," she said in affirmation.

"Pale colors are lovely against the bride's dress," she confirmed.

In addition, she knew every nook of the Townhouse floor of *The Mark* so she knew that the mantle in the Greenhouse would look lovely with a large but low vase of flowers. She also knew that the table with the seating cards arranged on it, at the top of the winding staircase, should have a tall vase of flowers. And of course she knew just where smaller centerpieces belonged on the café tables during the Reception.

But Marilyn really won my heart when she conveyed deep understanding of my request for a *chuppa* dripping with flowers. I had pulled a picture out of a magazine and Marilyn replicated it—every bit as thick and 'dripping' as I had requested. Soft, white tulle covered the frame and flowed down the sides like drapery, ending in a small pool of tulle on the floor. White and pink roses formed a thicket across the top of the *chuppa* and foliage continued flowing down the sides. And the tulle "drapes" were pulled back in the middle with a bouquet of roses. The shame was that the *chuppa* would be quickly dismantled as soon as the ceremony was over so the room could be prepared for the dinner. But flowers are ephemeral and that is part of their beauty.

11

Five Months Before the Wedding

Bridal Party:	Ask friends to be bridesmaids
	Select and order bridesmaids' dresses
	Ask friends to be ushers and name a Best Man
	Select mother-of-the bride/groom dresses
Invitations:	Select and order invitations

In this fifth month of preparation, the most challenging item is the invitations. Once the selection is made, the wording becomes very critical. Issues arise when there have been divorces and remarriages and ex-husbands, etc. One friend, to avoid the wrangling with the wording simply decided to omit all parents' names and the invitations seemingly came from the bride and groom inviting us to their wedding.

The mother-of-the-bride dress can be accomplished by the mother herself. Brides are stressed and have done enough shopping for their own dress. Also, they will be accompanying their bridesmaids in the search for dresses. Thus the mother's dress need not take center stage. Of course, if the bride wants to participate, she should be welcomed. Just make sure to find out what the bride really wants. Some brides want the mothers to wear matching colors; some want the mothers to match the color of the bridesmaids' dresses.

Bridesmaids are a lovely addition to a wedding. They enhance the ceremony, adding flavor and charm—and lots of laughter and loving support for the bride. I also think the guests enjoy watching young beauties saunter down the aisle. These sylphs can be accompanied by ushers, another handsome addition to the bridal party, or each can walk down separately.

Calling All Bridesmaids

My daughter's friends took such joy in being her bridesmaid. These young women clucked and chattered and schlepped and pondered. They took their mission in all earnestness and I was very impressed. They were Alexandra's bridesmaids and they were going to make her wedding their top priority! When I saw their genuine concern and witnessed my daughter's happiness in having them surround her, I first understood the deep friendships Alexandra had cultivated.

Armed with addresses and pictures and smiles and delight, we spent several Saturdays in pursuit. What color looked best on all of them—two brunettes, one blonde, one red-head? Was it ruby red or cranberry—what about wine? chocolate brown? Navy and black were definitely out! At this point, I was going to be either in brown velvet and lace or burgundy, depending upon which color Rebeca (the designer) could obtain from Italy. Should the girls "blend' with my color or be dressed in a totally different color? Alexandra, the calmest bride-to-be, was not concerned about color coordination, as long as the colors didn't conflict. If one of the girls wanted a strapless and the other wanted a halter top, it was fine with Alexandra as long as they selected the same color and the same material.

As we shopped, sometimes I walked a few steps behind, listening to their talk and watching them interact. It was delightful. To hear their ideas about life, about guys, about marriage. These were no naïve Bronx girls from the 1950s as I and my girlfriends had been. These were knowledgeable women brought up in Manhattan and "Sex and the City." Yet, there was also a naiveté simply because of their age. A refreshing innocence peeking through their sophisticated veneers.

"Umm, that looks lovely on you," Alexandra encouraged. "I see why you like that dress, but I think the 'Charlotte' is more flattering," she assisted her maid of honor.
"This size 2 is too big on me," Pam moaned to everyone's dismay. Who wouldn't kill to be a size two!!
Not to have the others upset, I pinched in the waist, "It's perfect on you!"
"I don't like this one as much as the two-piece," stated Alison.
"Well, sweetie, then you get the two-piece and the others will get the same style in one piece," Alexandra peacefully placated.

This amazing daughter has ever amazed me with her equanimity, her balance, her indisputable handling of possible disputes. She has never liked confrontation and early on learned the Socratic method. Why do you think you prefer this dress to the others? Can you see yourself in brown if we added a pink sash? What is it that seems to be pulling you to this one? Calmly questioning, encouraging each to reflect upon her desires, encouraging cooperation, and developing camaraderie among the disparate girls.

At some point during the day, I thought it was time to relax and have something to eat, cool off and break away from trying on dresses in stuffy salons. But, no, eating would make their tummies show. Water was the 'food' for the day.
We persevered. "Should we match the mother-of-the-bride dress," Amy asked. Alexandra didn't have any hard and fast rules as long as we all blended. Thus, ruby was a contender as it complimented the coloration of each girl's skin and hair.

On one particular Saturday, *Nicole Miller* was our first stop. Here they found a terrific ruby faille dress with a bustier top that laced in the back. The girls seemed to like this style but, of course, weren't ready to make any decisions yet. There were three other "houses" to explore and in the last place, *Serafina,* they decided on a chocolate-brown faille strapless with a pink grosgrain ribbon embracing their waists and trailing in a bow down the back of the dress.

After observing my daughter and her friends, and after six hours of taking pictures, smiling and approving everything, I decided I was not needed and kissed the girls good-bye. They were all going out to eat in Soho and I bowed out gracefully.
"Have fun, girls," I said kissing each good-bye.

I knew why my daughter loved these girls. They were so caring, accommodating, supportive and loving. It was Alexandra's wedding and they were thrilled for her. As I walked away I thought, "These bridesmaids are my daughter's best friends and if she wants, they will be her friends for life."

Each is delightful; each has her individual flair; each is quite different and yet my daughter blends with each one.

There is Alison who is not only a friend of Alexandra's but also her sister-in-law, as she was the friend who proclaimed, "You should meet my brother; you two will be great together!"

Alison has magnificent curly brown hair that she prefers to straighten. For years I paid exorbitant prices to have my hair permed to look like Alison's and here she is paying even more to have hers straightened. But curly or straight, she is alabaster skin, all curves, smiles and even-tempered. When the other girls were considering ruby, Alison cocked her head and said, "Ruby is good." When they changed to brown, she agreed, "Brown works." When Pam, long and lithe, moaned that the size 2 was too big, Alison laughed her good-natured laugh. Alison simply suggested that she'd get the same dress in a two-piece because she was more buxom. Whatever was decided upon she agreed. God bless Alison, I thought to myself.

There is Amy—thoughtful, dependable and serious. With her beautiful strawberry blonde hair and soft freckles, her ladylike demeanor and excellent taste, she seems to have just stepped out of a Henry James novel. She considered each dress the girls tried on, discussed the pros and cons with Alexandra and was deeply thoughtful about her decision. She also appears very calm, so it is easy to turn to her and ask for an opinion. She was going through a difficult time with a young man and it troubled me and Alexandra that while she was in the middle of a break-up she had to be involved in shopping for her girlfriend's wedding. Characteristically the lady, she put her personal issues on the side and was a vital participant in all that we planned. She was even more vital on Alexandra's wedding day when she took charge of a possible calamity.

Rachel is the only one who is already married, so she really understood what Alexandra was experiencing. Rachel is a 5 foot 2, bubbly, joyous young woman who brings cheer to everything. Her gorgeous smile challenges Julie Roberts' and her beauty surpasses that Hollywood star. Since she lives in Boston, she couldn't participate in our jaunts to the salons, but she followed closely on the Internet. When the decision was narrowed down between two styles, she found the comparable store in Boston and tried them on. Rachel became our time keeper—reminding everyone of the final order date, when the deposits were needed and when the pick up was ready.

Pam is a tall, lithe, blonde. She is the sensitive one, unaware of her sensuality and her beauty.

"I don't like my shoulders," she balked at the revealing dress everyone wanted.

"Oh, sweetie, you look beautiful," Alexandra reassured, as we all stared at the willowy, size 2 mannequin. Pamela is very creative and can not only paint but also can make desserts that should be on every Manhattan menu. Thus, she was going to create Alexandra and Adam's *ketubah,* a religious marriage certificate that is often framed and hung because of its beauty.

I imagined each of them getting married and know they'll have a wonderful (married) bridesmaid to count on. My daughter will be there at their weddings, assisting them with their gowns and their veils, remembering her own wonderful day.

The Honour of Your Presence

"I don't know what people talk about when they bemoan the planning of a wedding. It has been the most marvelous experience with me and my daughter," I exclaimed to all who would listen.

What did I know? I knew my daughter and I were good friends and could talk about any differences that might come up. I knew that my daughter and I had such similar taste, what could we possibly argue about? I knew Adam was flexible and easy going and as far as the wedding had few preferences. He really "got" it. "Weddings are for the bride," he said with insight.

What I didn't know was about invitations! I didn't realize how fraught with dissention the invitations would be. Even before the text, the major challenge of all, there is the style to select, the paper, and the font. That my daughter and her fiancé would want a classic invitation was never an issue. But for many couples and their "generation gap" parents, this can be the first major conflict. The choices, other than Crane's classics, are overwhelming. One can get family "seals" imprinted on the top, flowers all around the border, ribbons or stationery in rainbow colors.

What stock should be used? Do you like *Medici* or *Franklin Script*? Will you be traditional and select black lettering on ecru or modern and select a green stock with burgundy print? Do you like the one that has a thick ribbon wrapped around the middle of the invitation and tied with a bow in the front? Truly, not too major an issue.

"Should we have them done in thermography or have them engraved?" I asked.
"Oh, mother, they're only invitations. Let's use thermography. Engraving is so expensive," Alexandra responded.
I knew she'd say that and I knew I wanted engraved invitations. For me, they were the first connection with the guests; they set the tone. It was the *preamble* to the act.
"Black tie will tell them about the tone of the wedding," Alexandra said. "Besides, engraving is twice the price."
I ran to *Papyrus* to my new friend and advisor who agreed, "Engraving is so tasteful."
I now felt justified. My daughter acquiesced.

The next step was to have Adam come to the store and agree on all that we had selected. Yes, he loved the white paneled invitation, the script, the color ink. Yes, all was agreed upon. So far, all had been easy.

Then came the text. It is the text of the invitation that creates the first great minefield! Whose name goes where? Whose names should *appear*? Of course, in this liberal, anything-goes world in which we live, standards and traditions are often thrown to the wind. But if you like to abide by some standards you, like I, will find it hard to "go with the flow."

In no uncertain terms, the names of the parents of the bride appear on the first line of the invitation. They are making the wedding and it is they who are inviting guests and asking for "the honour of your presence…" If, however, the parents of the groom are sharing the cost of the wedding, both sets of parents may appear at the top of the invitation, so they say. I don't know who the "they" is, as such a guideline cannot be found in Crane's "*Wedding Blue Book: The Style and Etiquette of Announcements, Invitations and other Correspondence,*" the bible of the wedding invitation world. The parents of the groom, on Jewish wedding invitations, are placed below their son's name. I learned, curiously enough, that on Catholic invitations, the names of the groom's parents do not appear. How these "standards of decorum" came about is a mystery to most.

A real challenge is when there has been divorce and/or remarriage. What happens if one of the divorced parents is not participating in the wedding? Does the name of that parent drop off the radar screen? If the parent making the wedding has remarried, should the new mate's name appear? And how? What happens to the phrase "their daughter" since the new Mr. or Mrs. in the "Mr. and Mrs." is not the biological parent? And if it is the mother who has remarried, does her new last name appear, which will then be different than her daughter's? Then the question arises whether to include the daughter's last name as is done with the groom's name. Suddenly, there would be a lot of last names to completely confuse the guests.

And what if it's my scenario? What if the single parent making the wedding is with a man in her life to whom she is not married?
"Let's just put my name at the top," I suggested to my daughter as we perused the ten-ton *William Arthur* and *Crane* albums.

"But what about Leonard?" she queried.

I couldn't think anymore. I was getting tired. There had been too many things to think about, too many choices to make, too many contracts to enter, too much emotion to feel. At the absolutely wrong time, I decided not to think things through. Taking the easy way out, I assumed my easy-going boyfriend wouldn't care one way or the other.

Falling back on the bible, *Crane* advised that if I weren't remarried, I should put 'Mrs.' followed by my first, my maiden, and my last married name. That seemed simple. Except when the draft arrived and I looked at it, I could have cried.
Alexandra had a similar reaction, "Where's Leonard in all this, mom?"
"I don't know," I moaned.
So we went home to find out where Leonard wanted to be in all this.
"It's some time to first ask me," he said, hurt and sullen.
"You never care about such things," I accused.
"Who went to every wedding dress store with Alexandra? Who picked out her dress? Who went and interviewed bands?" he asked.
True. I had never connected the dots.

The next issue, then, was how to include a man's name, the most important man in my life whom I didn't happen to be married to at the time, but once was (huh?) The man who took Alexandra up and down the East coast as she interviewed with colleges. The man who bought her every beautiful dress she has in her closet, her first Louis Vuiton shoulder bag and the mirrored armoire she coveted. The man who took her with us on all our trips to Mexico. The man who taught her to *cha cha* and dance on two. That settled it.

So, our invitations read:

Mrs. Sandra Kyman Krystal
and Mr. Leonard Gurin
request the honour of your presence
at the wedding of her daughter
Alexandra Sara
to
Adam Lee
son of
Dr. and Mrs. Barry Hoffman

Saturday, the twenty-fifth of October
two thousand and three
at half after six o'clock

The Mark Hotel
New York City

Did I upset anyone? Probably. Did some people wonder at the inclusion of Leonard's name? Maybe. Just as I wondered at invitations I had received—like the one that excluded the second husband's name or the one that had no parents' names at all! I, too, had thrown *Crane's* etiquette to the wind. These days things are more complicated and I learned that each family makes its own rules, designs its own invitations and sends them out with the same joy and eager anticipation.

Couture for Sure

The mother-of-the-bride dress should follow certain guidelines. What they are I am not sure, since I have seen mothers of the bride wear black and some even wear white which used to be considered bad taste. Should their dress match those of the bridesmaids in color and/or in style? Is it proper for them to wear something low cut? I think the guideline is simply that the mother-of-the-bride should confer with her daughter and happily comply with her wishes. After all, every daughter wants her mother to look her best at this most wonderful event.

I didn't even want to bother Alexandra with the selection of a dress for me. She had enough on her plate and was working late hours and trying to remain calm. However, to my delight, she made time for me throughout the process.

Rebeca, a wonderful designer I had found through a friend, was creating a mother-of-the-bride dress for me that was a slinky velvet and lace affair that slithered down my body and ended in a mermaid bottom. The velvet strips, painstakingly placed, wound around my body in undulating waves. Not your usual mother-of-the-bride dress, I suppose.
"Go for it, mom," my daughter encouraged when she saw the sample gown. "You have the body—show it!" she declared.

When I had first seen the dress, I loved it. It was black velvet and lace with a soft, teal blue underlay that showed through the lace.
"Beautiful," I said, "but I can't wear black to my daughter's wedding."
Rebeca agreed.

Before deciding on color, she had to make a muslin pattern and place these sinewy strips around my body. It was a tedious affair. Four hours of standing on a little platform, in front of a mirror, as she and her assistant pinned thin strips around my body. Because they didn't simply go straight around, but curved, they had to be carefully placed to emphasize a hip, to show a waist, to cross the bust line in the right place.

My fittings ended up more complicated than the bride's. And then there was the decision of colors. At first I thought burgundy velvet and brown lace would be a glorious combination. Then we would have to add another color for the underlay and suddenly it began getting too 'busy.'

"What about blue, to match your eyes?" Rebeca suggested.
"What about brown velvet and brown lace with the blue underlay," my daughter suggested.

Having no time during the day, Alexandra accompanied me to Tribeca at night to help me select my colors. Exhausted from her intense days, she insisted on participating in the selection of my dress.
"That's what the fun is all about, mom. I don't want you picking out your dress all alone," she said.
And one night we spent two hours mixing five different swatches of brown velvet with a dozen different samples of blue under the brown lace.

"I never knew the range of blue," I wondered.
"This has too much taupe, in it. Dull," proclaimed Alexandra.
"She's right," Rebeca confirmed.
"This blue is beautiful, but will it show up when it's on the body?" I asked.
"Well, there'll be different lighting," Alexandra pointed out.
"She's right," agreed Rebeca.
What would I do without this wonderful daughter I thought?

They made the decisions. I no longer knew one swatch from the other. I am really not a detail person and this whole design thing was foreign to me. Whatever they decided I simply agreed.

When it was finished, I was no longer sure whether the dress was as beautiful as I had thought it would be. Too much time had passed and too many fittings had tired me out. After all that went into its design and production, I wasn't sure about the final turnout.
But others were.

You look like you were poured into that dress. It's gorgeous," Enid told me.
"You look incredible," another friend said.
"Magnificent," my girlfriend told me, as I whisked past her on the dance floor.
The mistake I made was asking my older sister, "Do you like my dress?"
"No," she said pursing her lips, "Sorry, but you asked."
"Why did you ask?" Leonard asked me in disbelief.
"I guess I was missing my mother," I joked.

12

Four Months Before the Wedding

Bride/Groom Attire: Order/buy tuxedo
Buy shoes
Begin the search for a tiara and veil
Buy cuff links and studs and cummerbund

Bridal party: Order bridesmaids' dresses
Buy/tuxedoes
Buy shoes and accessories

Beauty: Experiment with hairstyles
Meet with various hairstylists and make-up artists
for actual trials

Cake: Select wedding cake

Invitations: Choose a calligrapher and have him/her address
inside and outside envelopes

Out-of-Town Guests: Reserve a block of rooms at hotel

Honeymoon: Make reservations
Obtain passports (if required for trip)

Four months before the wedding is still an easygoing time. There is no pressure and most of the major decisions have been made. You have a dress ordered for all the women in the bridal party from the bride to the mother-of-the-bride/groom to the bridesmaids. You have the florist, the band, the photographer, the string ensemble and have ordered your invitations. Now you can experiment with your hair and your make-up, go to stylists and see how they work, look at pictures of hairdos and tiaras and have fun at make-up counters at *Saks Fifth Avenue* and *Bergdorf Goodman*. The list for "Four Months Before the Wedding" is hardly taxing.

The Four-Month Reprieve

By the end of June, much had been accomplished. I had checked off a good number of items on my "Lists." The venue, florist, photographer, band, and string ensemble had been selected and contracted, the bridal dress, mother-of-the-bride dress, bridesmaids' dresses and invitations had been ordered. And so there seemed to be a reprieve. But there really wasn't. Psychologically, it is all consuming.

You can think of nothing else but The Wedding. Your life is entirely informed by wedding preparations. I tried to read but had little concentration; in the middle of a sentence I would remember some item, some question and run to my folders and lists. When I'd look back to the page of the book, I was no longer interested. I had lost my place, my concentration and was soon, it felt, to lose my mind. Wedding, wedding—that's all I could think of.

"Vacation?" Leonard asked.

"After the wedding."

How could I leave, even for a week. What if something "came up?"

What came up in July was urging. Like a runner who hits a brick wall and can't go further, Alexandra was tired and it was summer. Suddenly, with the warm, sultry days she became languid.

"Ali, you need to find shoes."

"Ali, what about the tiara and veil?"

"Ali, you wanted to take a few dance lessons with Adam."

"Ali, you need to find a hair stylist and a make-up artist."

To each she replied, "Mother, there's plenty of time."

One weekend passed and then another but little headway was being made with my lists. I was at the *Four Months Before the Wedding* list and nothing was being crossed out. I couldn't select a tiara without her, I knew, but I could look for a veil.

On West 39th Street, the old millinery district, near the Garment Center that is sputtering out its last days, one can find a mixture of curious stores, most of which look as if they are going out of business. But don't be fooled. John at *Paul's Veils* makes the veils for the uptown salons but charges one third the price. So we got a silk chiffon, cathedral length veil, edged in ivory silk at a 66% discount.

My new ploy was to call her at work. "Alexandra, dear, I found a great tiara place. Want to meet me there during lunch break?"

Another lure I knew would work with my bargain-loving daughter was calling with the information, "Ali, Vera Wang is having a shoe sale. Want to meet me tomorrow after work?"

Now, mid July, the invitations were ready. All I had to do was take them to the calligrapher. We had decided that we wanted it done by hand, not on the computer, and fortunately found a young man who did beautiful work. When all the envelopes were addressed, I then had to insert the inserts into the right envelopes. Back to *Papyrus*, to my ever-helpful new-found friend.

"Cynthia, how do you enclose the inside envelope?"

"You know, no one has ever asked me that. Let's call *Crane*."

We learned that the direction and response card and envelope are placed with the invitation in the inside envelope atop the tissue that protects the invitation. This is then smoothly inserted into the outside mailing envelope—which is easier to say than do. The inside envelope was so full (with response card, direction card, response envelope) that I couldn't get it into the mailing envelope. Back to *Papyrus*, I have to admit, more than a little upset. For the cost of these invitations one would think they'd be generous with the size of the envelope!

"Cynthia, the outside envelopes are too small," I moaned.

This time she couldn't hide her amusement, "Your stock is so thick; this happens to all good invitations. It fits; just push gently but firmly," she advised.

The invitations lay on my glass table in the living room. They would remain there until the end of August. One should not mail wedding invitations more than eight weeks before the wedding; so I had to wait. But I wanted so much to mail them because that meant that I was actually making the announcement. It was so thrilling and yet so frightening. It was also conflicting. As long as they were not mailed, the wedding was not officially announced. Did I want to mail them? Did I not?

With all this seeming reflection, I still didn't really comprehend the portentous event. I looked at the envelopes with their beautiful calligraphy and still had little understanding of what was happening. I could easily say it and repeated it often to people, "My daughter is getting married." But I didn't have a clue as to what that actually meant.

I had been planning a wedding for eleven months and I truly had no idea what I was really doing. Yes, I knew I was selecting gowns and flowers and bands, etc. but I was going through the motions, planning, running, buying, selecting, deciding—for what I truly didn't understand. There is a knowing and there is Knowing. You cannot know what your daughter's wedding is—until it is. Of course, at this point, I did not have this knowledge even though I thought I knew exactly what I was planning for.

August came on the heels of a hot July with more humidity, more heat reflecting off the mica sidewalks, smacking New Yorkers in their sweltering faces.
"Let's get out of town," Leonard moaned.
"After the wedding."
How could I think of a trip?
Wedding planning permeates every cell in one's body; every neurotransmitter in the brain recognizes only those aspects that deal directly with this *one* event. Every thought and action is dictated by The Wedding.

A highlight in August was the cake tastings.
"Let's put a small amount of butter cream with chocolate mousse and combine it with a white cake," a petite woman with big black-framed glasses suggested.
"Hmm, this is delicious," we all agreed.
"Now let's try mocha and strawberry with the carrot cake," she offered.
There were four different kinds of cakes to choose from (white, chocolate, carrot and butter nut) and twelve different fillings that could be alternated in between the five different tiers. The choices became exponential and far too dizzying for me.
"We'll need to return with my step-dad and fiancé," Alexandra explained to this marvelously patient woman, a renowned baker of cakes for the famous and now for us. "Perfect, anytime."

"Mom," Alexandra oozed, "her flowers are the creamiest."
I had not even realized that they were edible. At our second round of cake-tasting, Leonard declared, "No contest," as he smacked his lips succoring the chocolate cake with hazelnut and mocha filling.

As August neared its close, I became anxious that the bridal salon had not called Alexandra for a first fitting. She, working out feverishly in the gym intent on losing a few more pounds, was perfectly complacent.

"It's fine, mom; there's plenty of time."

When Inga finally called for the first fitting, it had been almost 6 months since we had ordered the wedding gown.

"Does the train have lace on it?" I asked my daughter.

"Mother, how could you forget?"

The fitting was disappointing because it was only a muslin fitting and I still didn't see the gown! But the second fitting would be better, I assumed. For the second fitting, Leonard wanted to come also. It turned out that, for me, this fitting was little more than the first—only this time the actual satin was pinned around her body.

Leonard sucked in air, "Oh, it's gorgeous, honey," he told Alexandra, "You look so beautiful."

Alexandra looked in the mirror and whispered, "I feel like a princess."

I stood, staring. What were they going on about? A piece of satin hugged her body with large pins running up the back. Sans lace, sans train, sans satin buttons—and they both were slobbering about the gorgeous wedding gown.

I had spent the summer "reprieve" running around in the sweltering heat looking for the accessories. After the tiara and the veil, my daughter decided she wanted instamatic cameras on each table.

"Mother the ones I've seen on the Internet that are white are so cheap I know they won't take good pictures," Alexandra informed me. "The best are the Kodak ones, but they're black," she winced knowing I would wriggle my nose at this information. Black, plastic cameras on the beautiful pale pink damask linen with ivory bone china plates and lush-floral centerpieces all bathed in the light of soft candles! Never!

"We'll have to cover the cameras," I said firmly.

"How?"

So I returned to my haunt—West 39th Street with its warren of stores that for the most part looked as if they are momentarily going out of business. One battered-looking store held a cornucopia of trimmings and bindings and ribbons and silk flowers. Here they had just what I wanted—wide white ribbon that I wrapped around each camera, completely covering the black. Atop each ribbon-wrapped camera, I attached a soft, white silk lily.

The summer reprieve was over! I was exhausted and had headaches every day. This wonderful experience of making my daughter's wedding was wearing me down. I was thrilled that my daughter was getting married. More important, I had never seen my daughter so happy. That and her constant, "Oh mother, thank you so much for doing all this for me" kept me going. But it was such a dichotomous feeling. I felt so happy and so tired and the two feelings warred within me. And I was losing weight.

13

Three Months Before the Wedding

Wedding bands: Order wedding bands

Bridal Party: Purchase gifts for attendants

Beauty: Reserve hairstylist and determine hairstyle
       Reserve make-up artist
       Schedule appointments (manicure, pedicure, etc.)

Bride: Schedule wedding gown fittings

Honeymoon: Plan honeymoon wardrobe

Three months to go and most everything has been done. Nothing on the three-month list is daunting. But I need to be very honest with you, my readers. At this point, you are beginning to get a little nervous. You have been planning and planning for nine months but you're not sure how the wedding will really go. On some level, you're not even aware that your daughter is getting married. You have been planning and telling everyone but it really has not sunk into your bones. You know it only on a superficial level even though you have stated it often, "My daughter is getting married."

Wedding Bands: A Crash Course in Diamonds, Part II

If I thought there weren't too many choices for wedding bands, I was sorely mistaken. Here, once again, my gemologist had a lot to teach me.

I was flattered that both Adam and Alexandra wanted me to accompany them to look for the wedding bands. This go round Alexandra was not so sure about what she wanted but had to see the various choices on her finger. But she had done her research!

"A channel setting is when the diamonds are mounted in a groove that is carved out in the precious metal of the band; with a prong setting the stones share prongs so it creates a close setting and a clean line," she explained.
Adam just wanted to know how many diamonds she was talking about.
"Well, you can have five diamonds in the band that run along the top or you can have an *eternal*," she sighed.
I refused to be the one to ask what an eternal was, but Adam didn't flinch.
"Oh an eternal has diamonds that go all around the entire band," said Alexandra.

Adam had already passed the engagement ring challenge, so he didn't gasp too much when he learned that the 'eternal' was her desire. It was the size of each of the diamonds that was the question.
"I think point 20 is fine, don't you, mother?" she said reasonably.
"The point 25 look much nicer," Adam blurted out.
"And what's the clarity?" asked my gemologist daughter. "Is the color E or F?"

I could hear the jeweler's mental cash register ringing as we insisted on better and better clarity and more colorless color.
"After all," Alexandra declared, "it cannot detract from my solitaire."
She turned to Adam, smiled and said, "It's all right sweetie; we're only going on a one week honeymoon."
How that was supposed to assuage him I wasn't sure, but this young man so in love with my daughter was ready to purchase the Hope diamond if that's what she wanted.

If you don't know someone in the Jewelry Exchange, on 47th Street, you are dealing with danger. There must be some recommendation, some connection with a family member or a close friend. We were seated in a small room on the fifth floor of a building in the Jewelry Exchange. The diamond merchant was a youngish man, no *payes* or black hat, just a nice, Jewish, young man with whom another girlfriend's daughter had gone to school. This was the all needed recommendation. It's a "family affair" and although I don't really believe the prices vary that much, it's good to know the person has been in business for a long time and has done business with other people you know.

Typical of a diamond merchant, he had packets and packets of diamonds, with tiny hand-scribbled codes on each white wrapper. One wonders how they keep track of each of these little packets folded in half and half again. Their codes tell them what they paid for the packet and written on the outside is the size and color of the stones in each. For two hours Alexandra patiently looked through all his packets watching him measuring and weighing, asking questions, and selecting diamonds and placing them in a mounting that was a facsimile of the wedding band she would order. It was a wonder to me that she could differentiate between the coloration. After two hours, I could tell the difference between the point 20 and the point 25, but I had no clue about color. He could have done a three-card monte on me; I would not have known the difference. Alexandra knew exactly! Remarkably, she could tell the difference in one glance.
"These are definitely more an F than an E." The difference between a G and an H is so imperceptible that diamond dealers don't often agree.

Convincing this man that she would be his customer forever and promising to send all her single girlfriends to him when they became engaged, Alexandra then began to discuss price. I was her side-kick, agreeing and underscoring all that she said. Adam stood dumbfounded. He had never seen a team like us before. The diamond dealer weighed and made a mental calculation and wrote the number on a piece of paper which I thought was quite reasonable.

But Alexandra played her turn, "Can you make me a better offer?"
I held my breath. Adam stared, deadpan, and the suspense lasted for about 8 seconds.

Just count slowly to eight; it's a long time when you're holding your breath and hoping that you didn't whammy the deal. It's hard to refuse Alexandra and he made her happy with his final price.

When it was Adam's turn to select his band, it took fifteen minutes. He wanted a simple brushed platinum band.

14

Two Months Before the Wedding

Invitations:	Mail (6-8 weeks before wedding)
Reception:	Make tentative seating plans
Gowns:	Schedule bride's final fitting
	Pick up mother-of-the-bride's dress
	Pick up bridesmaids' dresses
Accessories:	Pick up veil
	Purchase tiara
	Bring in shoes to be dyed
Services:	Discuss details with photographer
	Discuss details with florist
	Discuss details with band
Ceremony:	Order yarmulkes
	Check marriage license requirements
	Finalize ceremony with officiant
	Order a ketubah

A One and A Two

Ask most people about a wedding and after describing the beauty of the bride, they will tell you about the band. The music truly enhances the affair and encourages the merriment of the guests; the more they get up to dance, the more fun they have. Thus, it is important to hire a good band as I have stated before.

Before the guests dance, however, there is the First Dance. Often the bride forgets to prepare for the first dance with her new husband. They have paid careful attention to the selection of their gown and their hairstyle and make-up and then they walk onto the dance floor totally unprepared for their first dance when all eyes will be focused on them. At one wedding I attended, the couple simply swayed to some fox-trot while the bride blushed probably praying for the music to stop. I witnessed another couple dancing very well, the bride's gown swirling as she revolved around the dance floor with her new partner stepping all over her dress. If you are going to be the only two on the dance floor, then you should make it look good. The first dance as "Mr. and Mrs." should be rehearsed and perhaps even a dance lesson or two is called for.

Alexandra was not going to leave one stone unturned.
"We have to practice our dance," she announced to Adam, "and Leonard can help."
Leonard was a terrific Latin dancer.

A one and a two and a cha-cha-cha. That's the beat we used at *El Patio Beach Club*, the summer of my 19th birthday. But that's not how Leonard danced it, he the *Palladian* pro. He danced on two.
"Bah, dah, bom," he would say, accompanying the bongo beat, "Do you hear it?"he would ask me. I was also supposed to hear the emphasis on the third beat. "No," I always responded. But I could follow well, so we looked good together on a dance floor. Well, as good as Katherine and Arthur Murray looked, I being 5'2" and Leonard 6'3".

The important solo dances for Alexandra and Adam's wedding were the first dance they would dance together and Alexandra and Leonard's dance. I was not going to do anything extraordinary when I danced with Adam's father and Adam was just hoping to get by with a foxtrot with his mom. But Alexandra wanted to dance a Latin number with Leonard, hardly your typical Father and Bride dance.

She loved moving her hips and shoulders and tipping her chin down with an upward glance and pursing lips.

To practice, we went to *La Maganetta*, a strange place on the Upper East Side, known only to Latin aficionados from the outer boroughs. The entrance-level restaurant is always empty but downstairs is where it's happening. Down the stairs is where the action is. The bands are live and loud and lively. Most of the time, we were the only non-Latinos there. It's a fun place where people come only to dance and strangers dance together and then part. This was our practice ground.

"Would you like to dance?" a man asked me. Without waiting for a reply, he put his hand formally around my waist and began leading me in the most gyrating mambo I had ever danced. It was wonderful; I thought I followed well. I have no idea what he thought because as soon as the music ended, he brought me back to my table with a formal, "Thank-you."
Alexandra, of course, was approached every dance number but was too shy to dance with a stranger.
"Ma, I'm not good enough."
"Just dance and you'll learn," I urged.
So she tried it once but was dripping wet when she retuned.
"That's too stressful, ma," she said and took Leonard's hand.

Alexandra got it—it was all those years of dancing in front of the mirror in my billowy skirts. She could dance on two. But she had to practice looking up and not down at the dance floor. "And smile," I told her. "You're supposed to be having fun."
Secretly, she must have been counting to herself to keep the beat. Leonard spun her out and pulled her in. He took her hand and led her sideways. They had their routine. Then they tried the *mambo*. Alexandra liked the faster beat, the sensual, fluid movements.
"Let's do a *mambo* at the wedding," she said excitedly.
And off they went—*bom, bad'dom bom, bad'dom*, moving across the dance floor. Looking like Ginger Rogers and Fred Astaire.

I was having a different experience with Adam.
"Lift your heels off the floor, sweetheart. You almost have to dance on the pads of your feet." I instructed.

"Try leaning a little forward," I suggested.

"Relax and move your hips," I added encouragingly.

But it was of no use. This trumpet-playing disco dancer found the Latin beat a challenge to his feet.

"Ma, I think Adam and I need to take a few fox-trot lessons. That's what we're going to dance for our First Dance," Alexandra said, ending my role as Katherine Murray.

Hats Off

Mazeltov.com was the site. When I called and was greeted by a voice machine, I should have been wary. "This is Malka. I'm not in right now but please leave your name and phone number." It turned out that Malka lived in Florida, so she probably was sunning at the pool or picking up her kids from school.

I was calling an Internet site to order yarmulkes, the little round prayer hats that Jewish men wear in temple and during wedding ceremonies. It is a minor task and I thought I'd get it accomplished quickly by ordering on the Internet. When I finally connected with Malka, she reassured me that they made beautiful yarmulkes in any color, choice of materials and had two different pipings.

Alexandra wanted black satin, unadorned. I thought that was too funereal so the next time Adam and she were at the house, I plopped a white yarmulke on his head. "Oh doesn't he look gorgeous with the white against his black hair?" Alexandra, of course, knew what I was doing. "Okay, mom, but no piping," she warned.

So I put in the order for white satin with silver piping. I thought by the time Alexandra saw the yarmulkes, they'd practically be walking down the aisle. Since it was now September and the Jewish holidays were around the corner, Malka promised to rush the order and I'd have them by the beginning of October. She was true to her word. They arrived. One hundred white yarmulkes with silver (ugh!) piping and inscribed:

Bat-Mitzvah
Alexandra Sara & Adam Lee Hoffman
October 25, 2003

There was a Jewish date under the secular one; if that was wrong as well I wouldn't have known. But I did know that my daughter and Adam were not candidates for Bat or Bar Mitzvah; they were being married!

"Don't worry," Malka assured me. "They made a mistake. I'll have them send new ones and you'll have them before the wedding."
At this point, things were beginning to be not so critical to me. "So, if we don't get them in time, we'll have a good laugh at the wedding," I said.

"Ma," Alexandra moaned, "it's not funny."
Sounding like Malka, I assured my daughter, "Don't worry; we'll have the right ones by the time of the wedding."

When they arrived, as promised, before the wedding, I wished I could return these as well. Now they looked so unfinished, without a trim. Should I have gotten the velvet ones? The silk moiré? Should I have ordered the ornate pattern with gold and red thread? I had thought a simple white satin would be tasteful. I decided it was too inconsequential and didn't refer to them again.

But I do have 100 yarmulkes sitting in a box in the back of my coat closet. What will I do with those silver trimmed hats announcing the *Bat Mitzvah* of Alexandra and Adam? I cannot throw them away. So I shall bring them out one day, on *Pesach*, and pass them around the Sedar table. It'll be a good laugh.

The Tree of Life

A *ketubah* is a 'contract' between the bride and groom to love and honor one another and to establish a home in the Jewish tradition. If you are religious it means to obey the laws of Moses, which are many. If you are not religious, it is a beautiful piece of art that you can hang in your home or simply put away in a drawer with your marriage license. I think when one is getting married, the idea of a *ketubah* arises because it is a tradition. And so you carry it on. Or you don't.

I did not have *ketubahs* for any of my marriages nor did I get a *get*. Perhaps that's why I had so much trouble when Herbert's cousin, an orthodox rabbi, wanted to marry us. All I had from my first marriage was that gorgeous Spanish written red-sealed paper—not a Jewish *get*. How was I supposed to locate Simeon or any of his family all of whom were mysterious and had unlisted phone numbers? Frantic phone calls got me one family member who promised to contact him. So Simeon, now living in Los Angeles, agreed to meet a rabbi on a street corner where the "ritual" was performed.

I found out what the "ritual" was when Herbert wanted a *get* from me. He coaxed and cajoled me to accompany him downtown to an office where I was greeted by three old, black-frocked, grizzly-bearded rabbis. Holding some symbolic object under my arm, I was instructed to walk around Herbert three times. I have no recollection whether I had to say something or whether they just muttered some archaic prayer and voila, I was divorced in the Jewish religion and free to marry again. Perhaps if I had had a *ketubah,* this *get* ritual could have been avoided. However, seven years later when I remarried, the rabbi never even asked me about a *get*. Again, I didn't have a ketubah made…or perhaps I did.

Beautiful *ketubahs* abound in New York City and can be purchased in various Judaica stores, the *Jewish Museum* or on the Internet. The choices of *ketubahs* are bountiful and are made in various mediums: prints, lithographs, watercolors, giclee, papercuts or handpainted. The designs are so multitudinous that I can hardly include all. They range from modern, such as Klimt's "the Kiss" with the Hebrew words "His left hand is under my head and his right arm embraces me," to the classic *Tree of Life* with arching branches that frame the text under a *chuppah* of colorful foliage, to Persian with scalloped arches and flowing geometric motifs. There is the *Ketubah of Acqui* that has two calligraphic borders richly decorated with floral and leaf patters. There are *ketubahs* with the Arch of Jerusalem and a rolling landscape of Israel. There is the popular *"Ani L'Dodi, Ve-Dodo Li"* Ketubah that translates to "I am my Beloved and my Beloved is Mine." There are Gardens of Eden with peacocks and flowers, Moorish elements, the Seven Species, Trees of Life with olive branches, symbols of Jerusalem, the Western Wall, fluttering doves and the Twelve Tribes.

Remember nothing is easy when it's your daughter's wedding. Of course, Alexandra wanted a *ketubah*; but she didn't want a manufactured one; she wanted an original. And her friend Pamela had offered to design a *ketubah*, so I had to find an undecorated *ketubah* that had only the text.

This time the site was 800ketubah and the woman was Nava. Like Malka, every time I called Nava, she was never home. Instead, I got her husband. I never found out what state she lived in or whether she was sunning or picking her children up from school. But it wasn't encouraging. Despite my yarmulke experience, I was going to give Nava a try.
"No decorations," she said, incredulously. "You want a *ketubah* with text only? Okay. Go to my site and select a text," she advised.

Easy I thought. When I went onto the website, I found staggering choices. There were:
<u>Traditional Aramaic</u>
Traditional Aramaic with English #1
Traditional Aramaic with English #2
<u>Conservative with Lieberman Clause</u>
Conservative #1
Conservative with English #2
Conservative with English #3
Conservative with English #4
<u>Reform</u>
Reform Hebrew with English #1
Reform Hebrew with English #2
Reform Hebrew Introduction with English #3
Reform Hebrew translation with English #3
Reform Hebrew with English #4
Reform Hebrew with English #5
Reform Canada

I began reading each, figuring out the differences among the several versions in each category. It began to get muddled and I must admit I never got to "Reform Canada."

In the traditional Orthodox *ketubah* text the groom undertakes certain financial obligations to ensure that his wife will be taken care of in the event that the marriage is dissolved. The wording was established in the Middle Ages and has not changed since. This one I liked. It was a prenuptial and they hadn't even known it—or had they? I thought it had possibilities.

The Conservative text is a 20th century modification of the traditional *ketubah* wording. It's the same as the Orthodox but has an additional clause (the Lieberman clause) in which the groom promises to give his bride a divorce should she ever want one. Lieberman, I surmised, must have been the father of Ms. Lieberman looking out for his daughter's well-being! However, since both the Orthodox and the Conservative *ketubahs* are written in Aramaic, very few people really know what they contain.

So the Reform text, written in Modern Hebrew and English, was looking good to me. The reform text contains expressions of love and commitment and each artist writes his own text so there are many variations to the wording. The Secular Humanistic text is appropriate for a marriage in which one of the partners is not Jewish.

After hours of reading the texts and taking notes, I called Alexandra with my "report." Before I could even begin, however, she said, "Oh mom I should have told you, I want traditional Hebrew no English at all."

I didn't tell her how I had just spent the past three hours. Why trouble my darling daughter who was under so much stress because she was getting married!

Two weeks before the wedding, a rolled scroll came in the mail and I brought it, unopened, to Pamela's house. The finished *ketubah* was not unveiled until the night of the wedding, when the rabbi and the wedding party waited in an antichamber for the 7:00 ceremony. There it was: both Hebrew and English text. Just as Alexandra had not asked for—but in the thrill of the moment (after all she was getting married in one half hour), she no longer cared.

More important was the oohing and ahhing over Pamela's design. Pamela had created a *ketubah* more beautiful than an illuminated manuscript. She had made a *Tree of Life* that reached up along the right-hand side of the *ketubah* with its boughs arched across the top and continuing down the left-hand side. On the branches she had placed tiny green leaves, hundreds of leaves, each hand-cut and pasted like a soft mosaic.

And the English translation began:
And on this thirteenth day of Tishre, in the year five thousand seven hundred and sixty four, the holy covenant of marriage was entered into between
        Adam Lee Hoffman and Alexandra Sara Krystal.
And they said unto each other: I take you to be mine according to the laws of Moses and Israel. We pledge to be equal partners, loving friends and supportive companions all through our life. We will value and revere one another with honor and integrity as we create a loving future together. We will bring out in ourselves and each other the qualities of forgiveness, compassion and virtue.

No prenuptial, no Lieberman Clause; no talk of a *get*—just an elaborate promise to love and cherish one another forever!

15

One Month Before the Wedding

Services:	Finalize details with band
	Tasting at *the Mark*
	Finalize musical selections for ceremony
	Finalize floral arrangements with the florist
Wedding Bands:	Pick up wedding bands
Bride:	Pick up shoes from the dyer
MOTB:	Pick up shoes from dyer
Transportation:	Choose and reserve car service to bring bride, etc. to the hotel

You are coming down to the wire. Now is the time when you must take care of yourself—your nerves, your sleep, your physical well-being. You are soon to become slightly unconscious of all that is happening which I suppose is a coping strategy that kicks in when a formidable event over which you have had almost complete suzerainty and for which you are mostly responsible is to occur. Despite this state of being, I do want to assure you that you have planned diligently and the wedding will go off wonderfully well.

The Dream State

There is very little left to do. And this is a blessing because at about this time a strange thing occurs to you. You enter a different state of being—one that you have never experienced before. A numbing takes over your psyche and you walk in a semi-conscious state. Like a zombie, you get up each morning, attend to your ablutions and somehow go through the motions of your day—but you are really not feeling. You are not thinking nor hearing and practically not breathing. You don't actually bang into things but you don't really see either. What has happened is that another person who looks just like you is present and you have gone far away. But this stranger who is you but not you is suddenly difficult to live with. She gets snappy, nervous, sappy. Other times, she is beatific, impenetrable, a stone statue. The strangest part is that no one realizes this and everyone continues to talk to you as if you were there.

"Mom, can you pick up my shoes?"
"Of course, dear," I answered in a far-off voice.
But I did manage to hail a taxi and remembered to tell the driver to take me to 83rd Street. I chatted with the Russian émigré who dyes shoes for all the top salons and has made Alexandra's white shoes a soft ivory. Do I remember how I got to his store? In some magical way, I got home.

I "coasted" in this semi-conscious state until the day of the wedding—when another major metamorphosis takes place (that for a later chapter).

"Surprise, we're coming to the wedding," my younger sister apprised me from Olympia, Washington.
"Oh, that's lovely. Of course, you'll stay here with us," I invited them in my dream state without thinking of what it really meant.

My younger sister who had run off to a commune thirty years ago was now coming back to New York with her ex-hippie, now Born Again husband who had never been to New York.
"What will you do with them for three days before the wedding?" Alexandra asked, already worried about me.
"I'll take them sightseeing," I said calmly.
"But mother, the wedding. You'll be exhausted by the day of my wedding."
"Oh, don't worry, dear," I said in my dream state.

"Aunt Sandra," my nephew Mitch called, "There's one less coming to the wedding. Helene and I broke up."

"Oh, that's too bad, dear," I said as if he had just told me Helene were going on a business trip instead of going entirely out of his life.

"Why don't you bring Jordan here on Saturday, so you and he can sleep over Saturday night?" I suggested. Jordan was his five-year old son from his third marriage.

"What about Shelbie and Jeremy?" he asked about his sister's children.

"They can sleep over as well."

"What are you doing?" Leonard asked. "You're going to have three children here the day of the wedding and then have them sleep over?"

"But I won't be here," I said calmly. "I'll get a baby sitter for them." And I dreamily walked into my bedroom.

Nothing was troubling me. Nothing could throw me. Remember, I was in my dream state. It truly was an indescribable state. I who am quite intense and need to plan things carefully was taking every new occurrence with the equanimity of a Buddhist monk. I had forgotten to perform my daily *tai qi* exercises and wasn't even practicing any *gigong* breathing but I didn't seem to need it. I was chill.

So I thought. What was really happening to me was inside, unbeknownst to me at the moment, and would become very obvious the week before the wedding.

Seating and Eating and…More Eating

In my dream state all I had to do was plan the table seating and select the food options for the reception and the dinner which was easily accomplished. They were not major challenges. First, I had only 55 people to seat; Adam's mother had the other 55 to place at round tables. For the selection of the food, I had four other people who were going to the tasting with me.

The Mark has a long banquet floor, with the dance floor in the middle.
"Let's mix the tables," Alexandra suggested, "so the guests from both sides of the family can talk to one another."

It was a lovely suggestion but the truth is that at a wedding, people want to sit near those they know. So on one side of the dance floor were six tables with my family (very few) and friends and Alexandra's friends. On the other side, were the Hoffman family and friends (many). I found an Internet site that had diagrams of various tables: round, rectangle, square. I printed out the round ones and figured out which tables needed eight and which needed ten.

Since we had asked people to respond by the first of October, I had three weeks to finalize the seating arrangements which gave me plenty of time. Of course, there are always possible cancellations, even though people have intentions of attending the wedding. The one I was most concerned about was my brother-in-law who was battling prostate cancer for several years and seemed, during the summer, to be losing the fight. Would he be able to sit in a car for two days and come up from Florida? The other was Adam's grandmother who, at 90, was deteriorating quickly. The emails flew back and forth with hope and hesitation. One of Barbara's friends was on "hold" because her daughter was expecting a baby and if it were a boy, she'd have to cancel on us to attend her grandson's *bris*. But Alessandro, the Catering Manager at *The Mark*, was very understanding. And we had until three days before the wedding to give a final account. So that part was easy. It was the worrying that was hard.

One thing we definitely didn't have to worry about was the food. Not the food from the *Mark's* 5 Star restaurant. We just had to select the dishes we wanted. "Another tasting?" Leonard smacked his lips, remembering the cake-tasting.

I gathered the group: Leonard, Jason, Alexandra and Adam. We sauntered over to *The Mark*, where Alessandro, several waiters and a sommelier awaited us. The fun began.

First we tried a few appetizers, each accompanied by an appropriate wine.
"Oh, the seared sashimi tuna is delicious," I mused.
"Beef carpaccio with goat cheese and frisee," Jason said.
Leonard declared, "Hands down, the duck confit."
Adam and Alexandra, the vegetarians, were leaving everything to us.

"Let's see about the second appetizer," Alessandro said as the waiter refilled our glasses of wine.
"I love the pan-seared porcini crusted scallop and oohm—chive whipped potatoes," I smacked my lips.
"Will anyone realize that it's seafood?" some one asked.
We all made believe we didn't hear the question.
"What about the quail with mascarpone polenta?" Leonard savored.
I voted for the seared foie gras with warm fruit sangria; Jason liked the wild mushroom risotto and so did the vegetarians.

"And what wine will accompany the fish appetizer?" my connoisseur son queried.
Then followed a discussion and tasting of three different French wines.
Since I shopped at Garnet Liquor, a great discount wine store in my building on 68th and Lexington, I knew wines in the $8-$20 category and bought according to one particular saleswoman's recommendations. I knew when a wine was too acidic for me and knew something about merlot and Italian pinot grigio. I even knew some French wines that came from *Cote de Rhone* and knew a *Medoc* or two. But I couldn't discuss wine like Jason could.

But I knew champagne! I had done some research, too! When I made the engagement party, I had learned about champagne.
"*Moet et Chandon Brut Imperial NV* is not bad, but for the special champagne toast I would like *Laurent Perrier Brut* which I think is better than *Taittinger Brut La Francaise*, although the Taittinger is more popular," I said simply—simply boastful.
My son's eyebrows raised, "Mom, I'm impressed!"

For the main dish, our guests would have a choice between meat or fish. Leonard convinced us all that beef was preferred over veal or lamb, so we all voted for the filet mignon. Alessandro was pleased because *The Mark* is noted for their aged, prime steak. He suggested a ragout of asparagus and mushrooms and pearl onion herb-roasted potatoes to accompany the succulent steak.

The tasting, it turned out, was a very complete dinner as each of us had a small portion of every item. By the time we got to the filet mignon, I dropped out. But I insisted on the wines! For the non-carnivorous guests, we had to choose among herb crusted salmon, tuna *au poivre*, or porcini crusted sea bass. The sea bass won hands down, even though there were only two people left in the tasting. Alexandra and Adam don't even eat fish.

At their wedding, while the guests feasted on sashimi tuna and filet mignon and sea bass, the bride and groom's menu was:

Mesclun salad, sherry vinaigrette
Herb risotto
Soy-glazed Tofu Steak
Baby bok choy

But they had the same dessert as everyone else: pear tart with port wine and vanilla ice-cream.

Ah, but before the dinner, there is the Reception. This is where you feed your guests before the dinner which doesn't make sense—but it's a ploy. While your guests are drinking and laughing and eating at the reception, behind closed doors, a race is occurring in the other room where the ceremony has just occurred. The chairs have to be pulled to the side, the *chuppa* has to be taken down as quickly as possible, and the tables, all beautifully pre-set, have to be taken from their hiding place (where do they keep them during the ceremony?) and placed accordingly on the floor. In the middle, the dance floor has to be put down.
"Can we do something with the flowers from the *chuppa*?" I had innocently asked the florist.
"Are you kidding?" she looked at me with wide, incredulous eyes. "Do you know how fast it must be dismantled? The guys just stuff the flowers into big trash bags."

It broke my heart to think of those beautiful petals mashed before their time, crushed and pushed into large, black plastic bags.

So, the only thing you can do with your guests while all this rearranging and setting up is occurring is feed them; ergo, the Reception. And I thought the reception was when you "received" your guests, as Queen Elizabeth does at all her events. Not done anymore.

There are options for the Reception. They're called stations! What are stations? Stations are more food. It's not enough to have butlered trays laden with delectable *hors d'oeuvres*. You must also give your guests tables of food with a carver or a server so there can be long lines of people waiting for their sushi or their carved roast beef. And this *before* the five-course dinner.

"Mother, it's a waste of money to have stations," Alexandra announced early on in our wedding planning, and I totally agreed with her.

Then something happens a few weeks before the wedding. You start thinking of other weddings and what was served—even though I eat hardly anything at weddings as I am so overwhelmed with the amount of food and underwhelmed with the taste. But when it's your daughter's wedding, suddenly you imagine your guests starving. After all, the invitation called for 6:30, the ceremony would end at 7:30 and dinner would be an hour after that.

"Ali," I called her at work, "I was thinking, maybe we should have a station at the reception."
She didn't balk at the suggestion this time which meant she had been thinking also.
"I guess it's a good idea," she confirmed.
"Alessandro, we've decided on stations after all." Through my cordless phone, I could see him smiling. He had known all along there'd be this change.
"Just tell me which you want," he said.

"You ordered two stations?" Alexandra questioned me. "I thought we had said only one."
"Honey, one looks chintzy. So the carving station will be in the *Greenhouse* and the sushi bar will be in the *Drawing Room.*"

16

Two Weeks Before the Wedding

Reception: Provide the final count of wedding guests
Finalize the seating plans
Have place cards made

Bride: Pick up wedding gown
Get hair trimmed

MOTB: Get haircut

Marriage License: Give license to Best Man for safekeeping

Payments: Balance to the hotel
Balance to the band
Balance to the florist

Beauty: Bride and MOTB get facial
Manicure, pedicure, waxing, etc.
Reconfirm with hairstylist and make-up artist

Scenario: Develop a scenario and email it to all members of the
wedding party so they will know exactly what the day of
the wedding "looks like"

Services: Finalize details with the band:
                                 What will be played for the first dance?
                                 What songs will be sung?
                                 What announcement will they make?
                             Finalize details with string ensemble:
                                 What selection will be played when each member of
                                 the bridal party walks down the aisle?

Although this list looks long, you really have accomplished most of it. There are some details to finalize, some balance of payments to be made but mostly it's picking up a few things and taking care of yourself.

And The Band Played On

Two weeks before the wedding and I was visualizing the evening, the flow, the dancing, the speeches, orchestrating the evening in my mind. I cannot emphasize enough that dancing is a very critical aspect of a wedding and all the details have to be agreed upon long before the evening. So I made an appointment to meet with the band director to firm things up and to confirm what we had discussed a year before when we had first signed the contract. No big deal, I thought. Except that the woman we had initially met seemed very changed. Oh she looked like the woman we had first met but her demeanor was definitely different.

Instead of the cordial, tactful business-woman who had seemed to understand who I was, we now couldn't communicate.

First she told us that the musicians needed to take a break every hour because of union rules.

"Well, that's fine," I responded, "but they can take these breaks one at a time and the guests will not be the wiser. We want continuous music."

"That's not how we do it," she snipped.

We were definitely dealing with a different person.

"Well, I think that's how we discussed it would be done for Adam and Alexandra's wedding," I insisted.

She clamped her mouth shut.

When it came to selections to be played and Alexandra handed her a prepared list, she said flatly, "That's not how we do it. You can tell us the type of music you want played and then we will play appropriate selections."

"That's not what we want," I responded.

At this point, things were definitely not going well and I quickly thought of the possibility of obtaining another band for the wedding. Then I looked at my daughter and decided I didn't want to upset her. So I used my collegial coaching techniques.

"I'm sure we can work this out. Let's give the list to the band leader and see if there are any selections that they don't know, so we can replace them with more familiar selections. Do you think this might work?"

She was forced, of course, to say, "It might."

But it was a very tight-lipped response.

When my dear future son-in-law asked, "At what point in the evening should we have the dance with me and my mother-in-law and Alexandra with my dad?" she put up another barrier.

"Oh, that's not done. I never heard of the groom having a dance with his mother-in-law—or the bride dancing with her father-in-law."

"But that's what we want," he insisted.

"We have been in the business for 30 years and we've done a lot of blue-blood weddings. And that is not done," she spit out.

I have no idea how I controlled myself. But when it's your daughter's wedding, you do. Adam came to my rescue and stated firmly, "Well that's what we want." After a few more items were discussed, we rigidly departed.

Never having had such an experience, I decided to speak to Alessandro about the meeting. He was quite surprised and asked if I wanted his boss to speak to her. I declined, thinking it best not to jeopardize the music at my daughter's wedding.

A few days later, e-mails flew back and forth between myself and this woman, deciding upon selections to play, finalizing the timeline, and all was in a very different tone.

Dear Sandra,
I don't want to hurry you but we still need the selection to be played for the Bride and Groom's first dance.

and

Dear Sandra,
I've gone over the program with Mike. Everything will be done as per the e-mail you sent me. I still need some tunes. Please advise.

and

Dear Sondra (*sic*)
I hate to be such a stickler, but I want to make sure we're prepared. I'll be there as well on Saturday. I think it'll be a great party!
Regards.

and two days before the wedding:

Dear Sandra,

I am also still missing a song for Adam and his Mom. Also, so Mike & I are clear, we are playing dance music as the Mark is serving the entree until the cake. Please correct me if I'm wrong.

Regards,

I think Alessandro definitely spoke to whoever it was!

Tense, Don't Ask

"You're unable to eat the week before the wedding," my friend Barbara warned me. She knew; she had made a wedding for her daughter just seven weeks before.
"That's okay, I don't eat much anyway," I said.
"Any other advice?" I asked her.
"Yes. All will be fine the day after the wedding."
That was comforting.
But she didn't tell me about the interim.

My dream state ended on the Monday before the wedding. Where had all the tension settled the last few months? It had been sneakily creeping around inside my body, in my bloodstream, through my nerve tissue, in my cerebellum and sundry other places.

Monday morning I awoke, looked in the bathroom mirror and screamed.
"What happened?" Leonard came running.
"My eyes, my eyes," I kept repeating. Under my pretty eyes, my beautiful blue eyes, were hanging two bags! My eyes were not just puffy—there were sacks filled with liquid. To attack the sacks under my eyes, I started with my *tai qi* exercises. Pointer-finger knuckles smoothing along the bone under my eyes, going from the inside corners to the temples. Breathe in and breathe out. One, two, three, four, five. Repeat: one, two, three, four five. Softly pressing as your knuckles gently pull along the bone. Nothing was happening!

When I called Yien Koo, my *tai qi chuan* teacher, she reminded me to "use my mind intention."
When I called Marcia, my non-spiritual friend, she suggested, "An antihistamine might help."

I tried the breathing first: breathe in through the nose, close the anal sphincter muscle and bring the *qi* up through your body along the spine, up to your hundred gathering points at the tip of your head, down through your third eye, slowly down through your chest, your abdomen, to your lower *dantien*, down through your legs, your feet and six feet into the ground.

On Tuesday I woke up, looked into the mirror and shrieked.

Leonard, less responsive to my screams, called out, "What's the matter, sweet thing?"

"A pimple; there's a pimple on the bridge of my nose."

I was more hysterical with the blemish (PIMPLE) on my nose than my water-logged eyes. Squeezing it, as we all know, is the worse thing to do. But something in all of us women urges us to squeeze just a little. Just a little, we convince ourselves, and it will subside. Of course, squeezing it made it bigger—and redder. Putting hot compresses on it at this point was useless; the only thing the hot towel did was burn my skin. I was a mess. I ran to my dermatologist's office desperate and crying.

"Hum, that does look a little vicious," he stated. And then he drew a picture for me, showing the pore and how it fills up with oil and debris and how when it is pressed between two fingers all one is doing is pushing the debris back into the pore. I looked at the upside down light bulb he had just drawn on the paper and cried even louder.

"Don't worry," he soothed and wrote a prescription for tetracycline, an antibiotic that is famous for causing thrush. That's all I needed, I thought, but I needed to get this pimple looking less vicious. It was Tuesday and I had only three days for the antibiotic to take effect. For good luck, he had me return in two days and injected the site with cortisone.

Add insomnia to all this. My dream state had ended; I now I couldn't sleep!

I was hysterical. Nothing like this had ever happened to me before. I who have survived four weddings and a funeral had never experienced such bodily breakdown as I was now. With all the stress in my life I had never had a blemish, an allergic reaction or insomnia. But for my daughter's wedding, I would experience all three.

I would lie down exhausted and fall asleep immediately but then, at 3:00 or 4:00 or 5:00, I would awaken, thinking of some aspect of the wedding. I'd go to my desk to write down what I had to remember the next day and then lie down again. But I couldn't fall back to sleep. Tick, tock. Well, no clock ticks anymore but the digital numbers kept plopping down: 4:43, 4:44, 4:45. This was crazy. I had to sleep! So it was into the kitchen, following my mother's tried-and-proven warm milk remedy.

Anne's Sleepytime Recipe

Place a little milk in a pot and put it on the stove on a medium to high flame;
When the milk starts to boil and rises to the tip of the pot, remove it from the flame;
Pour this molten liquid into a glass (not your good crystal as the heat might break the glass);
Let cool for a few minutes;
Drink it slowly feeling the warmth permeate your body;
Now, calm and quiet, return to bed.

Only this time it didn't work. Again, I started to break down. I need sleep. Some people can function on a few hours of sleep but I need at least seven hours or I cannot remain awake the next day. I started to panic. I had to sleep. I had four more nights to sleep before the wedding and I knew I had to get good sleep each of those nights or I would be a mess on my daughter's wedding day.

So I began my meditation. Sitting in a semi-lotus position, I began to relax. The same routine with the breathing—close the anal sphincter muscle and carry the *qi* through the body; to help clear my mind I counted from one to ten following the *qi*.
"Try a sleeping pill," Leonard suggested.

I have never taken a sleeping pill in my life and I do not believe in taking even a cold remedy pill. I believe in mind over matter. But I found myself, uncharacteristically, in the drugstore asking the pharmacist for a sleeping potion that would not kill me nor make me groggy the next day. He handed me *Unison* sleep gels, green rounds filled with diphenhydromine hydrochloride. It sounded suspect to me. I had always warned against drugs.
"If you can't pronounce the ingredients, don't take it," was my motto.
That night, against my good judgment, I hesitatingly placed the pill in my mouth and announced to Leonard, "I am taking a sleeping pill. I hope I wake up in the morning."

The next morning, like Scarlet in *Gone with the Wind*, I was happily stretching and smiling, snug in my bed. I had slept the entire night through. Now, I worried if I could take the pill for the next three nights. Or would I die. Bravely, I repeated it for the next three nights which probably saved me a great deal of angst.

By Saturday the pimple on my nose was imperceptible and, with a little cover up, no one was the wiser. The puffiness under my eyes had disappeared and by the end of the week, I was myself. Well, almost myself. I had to survive the wedding day!

PART III
The Event

17

Day of Wedding

Payments (checks):   Balance for the string ensemble
Officiant's fee
Balance to the photographer
Balance for the hairstylist and make-up artist

Bring to the hotel: Emergency kit
Kiddush cup
Yarmulkes
Cameras
Place cards
Gowns and accessories (stockings, undergarment, shoes, make-up, evening bags, jewelry

Wedding rings (usually the best Man is given this responsibility)

Beauty: Mother-of-the-bride goes to beauty salon for a blow out
Bride has her hair and make-up done with specialists

It's actually here—the day of the wedding. You have been planning this for one year of your life and it will be over by night's end. Of course, you must get through the day first—the dressing, the picture taking, the rehearsal. But the actual wedding, ceremony, reception and dinner/dance will be but a memory after 5 ½ hours. Amazing!

To make sure that all your planning will not go down the drain in missed cues, wrong timing and other mishaps, I strongly suggest that you envision the day and the evening and create timelines. It's your script. After all, a play cannot be performed without a script. And you are the director.

Timelines

As the director, how do you think things should flow? What should occur first? second? and so on. It might be easier to discuss this aspect in terms of time. There are two different timelines the day of the wedding. The timeline for the day of the wedding is established by the bride in collaboration with the photographer. The timeline for the night of the wedding is established by the catering manager where the wedding will take place.

Daytime Timeline

About two weeks before the wedding, it's a good idea to begin to visualize. The bride might want to think about the following:

How do I want the day to flow?
When will I go to the hotel/venue?
When should I have my hairstylist arrive to do my hair?
Will my bridesmaids use the hairstylist as well?
When should I have my bridesmaids arrive?
How should I coordinate the make-up artist?
What time should I get dressed?
When should the groom arrive? the photographer? the rest of the wedding party?

Since Alexandra's desire was to have pictures outdoors, it was planned that she and Adam would go with the photographer, at 3:30, to Central Park and have an hour alone; then the wedding party would arrive at 4:30. We all had to be back for the ceremony rehearsal at 5:30.

Our timeline looked like this:
10:30 Sandra goes to beauty salon
11:00 Car picks up Alexandra and Sandra and brings everything to *The Mark*
11:40 Arrive at hair stylist who begins working with Alexandra
11:40 Make-up artist begins working with Sandra
12:30 Alison, Amy (bridesmaids) and Barbara (MOTG) arrive
1:45 Alexandra and Sandra are finished and go to *The Mark*
2:00 Alexandra rests (?)
2:30 Pamela and Rachel (bridesmaids) come to *The Mark*
2:30 Photographer arrives and takes pictures of Alexandra preparing

3:00   Adam, Leonard, Jason, Joshua, Barry and Danny arrive.
        Adam, Alexandra and Rob (photographer) proceed to Central Park
3:00   Wedding party "chills" at *The Mark*
3:45   Wedding party goes to Central Park
5:00   Everyone returns to *The Mark*; relax
5:30   Rehearsal
6:00   Rabbi arrives—Ketubah signing, etc.
6:30   Sterling Music Ensemble arrives
7:00   Ceremony

Evening Timeline

The evening timeline is a little more complicated. You need to create time slots for each segment of the evening: the arrival of the guests, the ceremony, the cocktail hour, the dinner/dance. Within each, you should further refine the time parameters into subsets. For example, as we outlined the timeframe for serving the appetizers, the main course and the dessert, we had to intersperse the first dance of the bride and groom, the dance with the bride and her father, the welcoming remarks, the Best Man's toast, etc. You want a good flow. You want your guests to be comfortable. It's important to visualize your guests eating their appetizers. How long do you think this will take? What music should be played for this period of time? While the plates are removed from the tables and before the next course is served, there will be time for your guests to dance. What music would you like the band to play?

I keep emphasizing how important music is, as it helps to set the tone of the entire wedding. At too many weddings, I have sat at a table unable to converse with the person next to me; the music was blaring away. You need to discuss with the band about the "balance;" you want the music to be lively but that does not mean shattering the cilia in everyone's ears. You might also want to think about when there should be softer, traditional music so the older guests can dance and when the more lively music should begin. I suggest mixing the styles but here is where your bandleader should pick up cues from the crowd. If they're playing a slow number and no one is getting up to dance, they should switch to another genre.

Our Evening Timeline

6:30 Guests arrive
7:00 Ceremony
7:30 Cocktail reception in the *Greenhouse* & the *Drawing Room*
8:30 Direct guests to *Mark Suite* for the dinner/dance
8:35 Take orders for the main course (offer both red and white wine)
8:40 Introduction of Bride and Groom for First Dance
8:50 *Hora*
8:55 Welcoming Remarks (MOTB)
9:00 Blessing of the *Challah* (decide who will say the prayer)
      Blessing of the Wine (decide who will say the prayer)
9:05 Serve appetizer (dance music)
9:25 Dance Set: Bride and Father
                      Groom and Mother
      Guests are invited to join the dancing.
      Wait staff pours the champagne
9:40 Best Man's Speech; Champagne Toast
9:45 Serve Second Course
      Dancing to be continuous throughout the second course.
10:00 Dance Set: Groom and Mother-in-Law
                      Bride and Father-in-Law
10:15 Serve main course (continuous dancing)
11:00 Cake Ceremony
11:10 Serve Dessert, coffee and tea (dancing resumes until the end)
11:30 Serve Wedding Cake
12:30 Conclusion

Emergency

What emergencies might occur at a wedding? Hopefully, no one will get sick but just in case, you might discuss with the manager what happens if, for example, someone faints or falls ill?

On the lighter side, there are little emergencies that can be avoided by preparing in advance. Perhaps you want to have an extra pair of stockings in case one pair gets a run. Headache anyone? Do bring any medication that you might have to take.

Butalbitol (headache pills)
Band-aids
Hair dryer and flatiron (for hair)
Hairspray
Little scissors
Tweezers
Extra pair of stockings

Oh, how I wished I had followed my own advice and included a needle and white thread!

The Day

All week I had implored, "Please dear G-d, let the sun shine on Saturday." I spoke to Him several times each day, bargaining and making various deals so He would grant my daughter a beautiful day. My daughter had her heart set on taking pictures in Central Park. Rain was not negotiable. But I had no powers over the elements and I moaned at my impotency. Each morning for a week before the wedding, with my heart in a grip, I listened to the weather channel. Cheerfully, these talking heads gave forecasts of drizzle or possible chance of rain. It was a cold, dreary week. On my knees, I asked God for only one day of sun, Saturday, October 25th. If it then rained for forty days and forty nights I would not complain.
"Just make this one day sunny for my daughter—for her pictures in Central Park."

Nature heard me. October 25, 2003 was a beautiful day. The sun was shining and the temperature was in the high 50s, a perfect October day. But I was too tense to truly appreciate the sun, not that I wasn't grateful that my prayers had been answered. But now I was worrying about the next thing and another malady occurred. I could barely talk; my jaws seemed to be locked in preparatory fright.

I walked the few blocks to Madison Avenue to my hairstylist who was only going to wash my hair and blow it dry. Usually late, she was there on time. Often during my haircut she is upset with something in her life; this day she smiled softly. Usually, we gaily chatter; this day we were stone silent. She knew-she is very intuitive. Only our eyes locked and communicated. She did my hair perfectly!!

When I arrived back at the house at exactly 11:00, the car was there and the doormen were loading it up—wedding dress, my dress, veil, tiara, shoes, pocketbooks—everything Alexandra would need. Off to *The Mark* where our things were placed in the suite. A turn around the corner to a lovely townhouse on 78th Street brought us to the hair stylists (there would be three) and the make-up artist. And here my tension blossomed. Too many people and too much activity. Two of the bridesmaids and the mother-of-the-groom joined us and it became noisy and hectic with everyone concerned about her hair and make-up.

"Hey, this is Alexandra's day," I wanted to say but remained mute.
And there was Alexandra assisting her friends.

"Oh, your hair looks so lovely that way," Alexandra encouraged.
But no one was worrying about her hair. I looked at the hairstylist wrapping Alexandra's hair around a "rat."
"The bun is too big," I managed to say, "I think it needs to be a little smaller."
"That's all right, mother, Alexi knows what she's doing," Alexandra said.

Then I paid attention to what the make-up artist was doing to me!
"This is too thick; you have to separate the lashes," I panicked.
"Yes, of course," he assuaged as the mascara dried harder and harder on my clumped lashes. When he picked up a red lipstick, I knew I had to get out of there. Make-up artists always want to put red on my already full lips accentuating them beyond belief. I grabbed his hand in mid air, "Stop," I screamed.
"Perhaps you should use my mother's lipstick," Alexandra suggested.
"Honey this is too much for me. I'm going back to *The Mark* and I'll wait for you there."
As I departed, I said tight-lipped, "Take care of the bride everyone!"
I'm sure I wasn't too popular that afternoon.

Alexandra walked into the suite at about 1:30. First, I caught my breath; then I cried. She was so beautiful. My statuesque beauty was more beautiful than ever. Her hair was pulled back in an elegant bun and she looked like an alabaster statue of Queen Nefertiti.

Now it was time to dress the Queen.

First, I took the gown out of its "encasement" that had held it hanging from the high joint in the door of the den/bedroom, like an altarpiece. As the gown was unveiled, a hush came over the suite. All eyes were on the crisp Duchess satin gown with fifty satin buttons that now had to be buttoned. Alexandra stepped into the gown and I zipped it up. Next were the buttons. In horror, I saw that the first button was missing! The gown had been in my safe keeping since it was ready in mid-September. I had watched over it like a mother with a newborn babe. Leonard had not been allowed to smoke a cigar in the house lest the odor permeate the plastic covering and ruin the dress! I had unzipped its specially designed garment bag, so the dress could "breathe" and not, G-d forbid, get creased. But I had not checked the buttons!

Now on her wedding day, just five hours before she would walk down the aisle, a button was missing. I flashed a glance at Amy which she read correctly as, "Should we tell Alexandra?"
Her look told me not to say a word so I began to button the dress. But my heart gripped. The first button I attempted fell into the palm of my hand!
"I need a needle and thread," I tried to sound calm and in control.
"The emergency kit," Alexandra suggested.

In planning the emergency kit, however, I had decided not to include a needle and thread thinking no one would have her wits to sew anything. Instead I had brought safety pins. Now we needed needle and thread.

Needle, thread. "I need a needle and thread," I now called out hysterically.

Alexandra stood, still. She was not going to let my hysteria effect her demeanor. Everyone repeated my request for a needle and thread. Suggestions came. What about the drug store on the corner—*Zitomar*, they had everything. Let's get the concierge to buy a needle and white thread. What about housekeeping at the hotel? They must have needle and thread.
"But I need it *now*!" came through clenched teeth.
"Here's needle and thread," a voice said.
Seemingly out of no where but with the gravity of an assistant in an operating room, Rob, the photographer, handed me a small, plastic sewing kit with several needles already threaded. A photographer with needle and thread! I began sewing, my hands shaking and fumbling. It was all too horrible. One calamity after another. As soon as I began to sew the button, I pricked myself. Blood! *Blood* on my daughter's wedding dress! I was past hysterical now.
A fairy princess calmly took the needle and thread from trembling hands and without saying a word, the Good Fairy was sewing. Amy, who shops at *Bergdorf's* and sleeps on *Frette* sheets was *sewing*. Where did she learn how to sew? I have never asked her. I have just blessed her every day since.

Next was the tiara. I was to place the tiara exactly where the bun began and where the veil would be attached. But where was the tiara? We all began to open drawers, look under sofas, chairs, the bed. We searched through the antechamber, the kitchen, the marble bathroom, but there was no tiara.

"Let's retrace our steps," Alexandra guided.

"Amy, you took it out of the box and then…mom, didn't you look at it?"
"I put it back in the box," Barbara said defensively.
"Mother please find my tiara," Alexandra, for the first time, looked sadly at me, imploring me to make everything all right.

Oh, the sandbox, the sandbox. It was so easy to make everything right in the sandbox days. Now I had to find a lost tiara.
"The hairstylist had some lovely tiaras. She'll definitely let you use one," I offered.
"But I want my tiara," Alexandra was almost in tears.
"Don't cry sweetheart, your make-up," I reminded her.

In my sweep of the suite, I returned to the bathroom, which had three separate rooms, one leading into the other with the deepest being the one with a Jacuzzi bathtub and the toilet. There lying on the floor scale, was the box. I had found the tiara!
"Who went to the bathroom and took my tiara?" Alexandra wondered.
I never told her it was I!!!

Alexandra's plan was shot. "Mom when Rob comes to the hotel, I want him to take pictures of me being dressed, maybe you putting the tiara on my head," she had planned. That was out now. My face was gripped in a vise and my eyes were desperate. We took none of the pictures of me dressing Alexandra in the suite.

On schedule, the bell rang and there was Adam—all ready to go—except his bowtie.
"Who can tie this for me?" he asked. Jason attempted to assist his almost brother-in-law but his own tie was cockeyed, so Alexandra did it. And off they went to Central Park. She called over her shoulder, "Mother it's time you got dressed!"
I could now breathe—my daughter was dressed and happy. I was making her dream come true.

The worst was over. Alexandra's gown was buttoned, her hair was up, her make-up was on and she looked beautiful. More important, she was so happy. She and Adam were in a private sphere. They were with us, but, simultaneously, they were off on their own. They looked adoringly at one another, they clasped hands, they cooed and they kissed. I exhaled as they floated out the door.

Now that they were off, it was "rest time" for the remainder of the wedding party—that's what the scenario outlined. Since we had an hour before we were to join the bride and groom, I grabbed Leonard. We went down to the bar, nestled in the corner of the lobby, and I nestled into his chest and ordered a vodka on the rocks.

"Relax, sweet thing. Everything is perfect," he reassured me.

Alone with the rock of my life I was not tense and it was the only time during the entire day that my jaws relaxed and my breathing was normal. What happened to my *Qigong!*

Central Park, like the weather, was perfect that day. The leaves were still green and full on the boughs and the trees looked especially tall. The elms stood like sentinels, the maples swooped low almost caressing our heads and the clear, crisp air gently touched our bare shoulders. For an hour we took pictures and it was another segment of the day when I was able to relax and really laugh.

Oh the pictures we took. All permutations—Leonard and me and Alexandra, Leonard and me and Alexandra and Adam; Leonard and me and Alexandra and Adam and Jason; Alexandra and me; Alexandra and Jason; Adam with the girls; Adam with his brothers and sister; Adam and Alexandra; Adam and Alexandra with Barry and Barbara; Alexandra with her bridesmaids. Laughing, posing, candid captures, hugging, holding. Two months after the wedding, we had 1000 perfect pictures from which to choose.

The Wedding is Here!

Imagine now that it is the night of the wedding. In a few minutes you will hear your musical cue and you will take your daughter's hand to escort her down the aisle. The doors will open and there will be the invited guests all looking at you and your daughter. You will begin the magical evening in a semi-dream that will end only when your head hits the pillow much later that night.

But first the event!

The ushers marched swiftly and assuredly down the aisle. Jason swung down the aisle even managing to smile at the guests. Adam was excited when he heard his cue, *The Prince of Denmark*, and he pulled his parents forward. No lamb to the slaughter, he. Happily he walked down the aisle and in great anticipation took his station at the center of the *chuppa*, where the rabbi stood, waiting for his bride.

The bridesmaids sauntered one by one, holding their bouquets of fall flowers, burgundy and pink calla lilies and roses, exquisite in their cocoa strapless dresses with a pink faille ribbon circling their waists. First Amy, with her strawberry hair softly encircling her face, smiling demurely, pacing herself perfectly to the violin strains of *Salut D'Amour*. Next came Pamela, tall and lithe, her soft blonde-brown hair cascading down past her shoulders, eyes demurely downcast. Rachel followed, bright and electric, her hair in a sleek updo, seemingly enjoying this walk down the aisle. Then Alison, with her proud and sure step, pranced down the aisle, smiling from ear lobe to ear lobe. What a preamble to the Act!

Then there was a pause, a hush, as the staff rolled out the white brocade carpet for Alexandra. With the first strains of the *Intermezzo*, Allegra and her ensemble called to us. I grasped Alexandra's hand and took a deep breath. It was a rather long walk down the aisle. There was much to see and little to do except stare. When I looked up at my daughter, she had her eyes fixed straight ahead, on Adam, waiting for her at the *chuppa*. I, on the other hand, wondered what I was doing. I looked around and saw familiar faces. There was my friend Helene and there was Enid. Oh Cousin Steve, I'm so glad you're here. Their eyes caught mine and suddenly I thought it rude to just stare back at them. So I began to say "hello" to one or two. There I was walking my daughter down the aisle—"giving her away" as the expression goes—supposedly involved in one of the most solemn acts of my life and I was smiling and saying 'hello' to people. When I saw my friend Irene, I whispered, "This is like a dream." Alexandra's gaze was held steadfast on Adam and her mother was yakking away!

Somewhere in my consciousness I was aware that this was the climax, the moment for which all the preparations had been made. But that was some vague thought reeling around in my brain. Simultaneously, I wondered who this magnificent creature was. I was holding a young beauty's hand…who was she? This majesty smiling gorgeously, walking towards her Prince. My only explanation is that an Imposter had taken my place. Thus, the person walking down the aisle had no idea what she was supposed to do and didn't even know the Princess at her side.

We stopped two feet before the *chuppa*. Leonard, on cue, came to my side and stood there. Suddenly Sandra was present. I knew I had to function now. Leonard kissed me but had completely forgotten what he was supposed to do which was to take Alexandra's hand and put it into Adam's. So I gently pulled him to my side (not so easy to gently pull a 6'3", 240 pound man) and Adam walked up to us. I took Leonard's hand and placed it on Alexandra's and Adam took her hand. Then it seemed we didn't know how to part, so there was a lot of kissing (all unrehearsed). I kissed Alexandra; Leonard kissed Alexandra; I kissed Adam; Adam kissed me. I don't think Leonard kissed Adam. The guests had to be thinking, "Is this kissing ever going to end?"

I watched the ceremony with interest, a dry-eyed spectator. I who cry when I see any commercial that has to do with family wasn't shedding a tear at my own daughter's wedding. I watched her walk around Adam three times, I listened to what the rabbi said about their union and I smiled. I had been smiling so long that my cheeks felt a little tired but I couldn't seem to stop. When the rabbi asked them to put their heads close to each other and they closed their eyes and he blessed them, tears did well up, but I didn't cry. When Adam crushed the glass, signifying that they were man and wife, I finally experienced a seismic jolt and first realized what this wedding and a year of planning was about. It was my first recognition, on some conscious level, that my daughter was getting married which meant she was part of a union with a man. But I still didn't cry. It was so joyous—certainly not the time for tears. Or maybe I was just numb.
The recessional played and we happily walked back up the aisle and out to *The Greenhouse* to receive our guests. Now the fun would begin.

The rest unfolded easily. The dancing and the toasting, the eating and the dancing. I floated through it all, a part of me observing everything from above. There the Imposter was again, on the dance floor. Whom was I/she dancing with? I/She was laughing, smiling. What was I/she saying? I was floating out in space wondering why this party. Looking down at the throng on the dance floor, I smiled contentedly feeling that everyone was having a good time and knew that no one was missing me. They thought I was there! Invisible, up in the air, I had the opportunity to wonder why, now that Alexandra and Adam were man and wife, this last coda had to be enacted. Why didn't the play end when the ceremony did? For me that would have been perfect. How nice of you to have come. Thank you. Goodbye.

Instead, there was the Imposter acting as the hostess of this large party.
"How are you?"
"You look wonderful!"
What a great dress!"
"Do you have a drink?"

And the Imposter began doing the silliest things. She danced with my sister Lynne and hurriedly ran and took the hand of my younger sister Marilyn, directing her to the dance floor to include her in the dance. Then she even remembered to include Barbara, my *machitenim*. So she ran and pulled her to the dance floor. Like a professional party host, she went through the motions, smiling and appearing as if she were having a marvelous time. And amazingly, everyone thought it was I.

When the emcee introduced me, the Imposter calmly walked up to the podium and gave *my* welcoming remarks. How had she known what I wanted to say? Well-practiced, she thanked everyone for coming and enumerated a few important people who had made special efforts and long trips to attend. She thanked Alexandra's friends and didn't leave out a name. She delivered her remarks with humor and then read the poem I had written. How did she know my poem? I had written it on loose pieces of paper in the middle of several nights whenever I had had another thought. And there was the Imposter delivering it with great aplomb. She was stealing my part at this point. But then I realized how wonderful she was to have stood in for me when I was so far away. I laughed at the joke being played!!

After the Ball is Over

I cannot explain, without sounding horrible, how delighted I was when the wedding was over.

"I felt so let down the next day," Irene had told me.

"I planned a trip so I wouldn't feel down after the wedding was over," Barbara said.

Friends told me they had felt adrift for quite a time, after their child's wedding was over. Forgive me dear Alexandra, Adam and dear friends. I clicked my heels! I sang; I jumped. No, I whooped! It was over! I could breathe again!

Free—I could go back to my life and partake in it. I could work out in the gym and develop my muscle groups; I could go to the museum and pause at a painting; I could read a book and develop my mind. I could be me again. I could feel and sleep and eat and laugh and live my quotidian days—the days that I love, now that I am free from constraints and time frames, jobs and responsibilities.

I am so thrilled that my daughter is married to a wonderful, loving young man who has become so deeply a part of our family. He still ends every phone conversation with, "I love you." I love every moment that we are together and we are together often. They loved their wedding and thought it was perfect. Far be it from me to disagree or point out anything that wasn't perfect. I am thrilled that I was able to give that night's memory to them.

Perhaps I could have lived very nicely without the wedding! Perhaps a small group of twenty or thirty people gathered in a beautiful temple. Just enough people—the closest friends and loved ones—to witness the rabbi blessing the couple and announcing them Man and Wife. Then perhaps a lovely dinner in an elegant restaurant—why, the restaurant in *The Mark* would have been great. I could have worn a smart Prada suit and Alexandra could have bought a beautiful soft silk dress, even off-white if that was her desire. Or even a caviar and salmon buffet, in my house, with champagne flowing, toasts and warm, intimate laughter. Oh, dear. The latter describes my wedding to Leonard. This was what I had thought perfect for my fourth wedding to the one beloved of my life.

Hmmmm…so Alexandra had been right. She and Adam had to have a big wedding. They had to experience all that such a wedding encompasses. The big wedding is for the young, the innocent who look toward their future with dewy-eyed optimism. The wedding with "all the trimmings" must occur when it will be the wedding of their lives. No sending off your daughter in a paltry fashion. There must be a long Princess gown and a *chuppa* dripping with pale roses. There must be dinner and dancing so that everyone will remember with delight the night that Alexandra and Adam became man and wife.

There must be reminiscing, recalling the most wonderful affair enjoyed by all. There must be pictures of a beautiful bride and her handsome groom kissing in Central Park, happily marching down the aisle, dancing their first dance as everyone encircles them clapping and smiling and calling "*mazel tov*." There must be the pictures of the bride and groom precariously perched on chairs held high above the heads of the wedding guests, rotating to the tempo of the *hora*.

These are the memories that must exist! The slight insanity that goes into spending a year planning a wedding for a six-hour event is something everyone should experience. Crazy? Yes. But a wonderful crazy at that!

The wedding gown is hanging in a closet in my den; I'm not sure what Alexandra wants to do with it. I will bring it in to be cleaned…soon. My gown is hanging right next to hers, the hem down and the velvet crushed. I will call Rebecca and have her put it "back together again"….maybe. The *ketubah* that had seemed so important for Alexandra to have is rolled up, also in the den closet. Alexandra will frame it…whenever. My folders filled with pictures of flowers and tiaras and wedding gowns and my lists will be thrown away…soon. Or, perhaps, not.

Life is memory. And your daughter's wedding is the best memory of all. Especially when you have made her dream come true.

Appendix A

Musical Selections for Dancing

Our list to the band was the following:

Twist and Shout
Papa Don't Take No Mess (James Brown)
Chameleon (Herbie Hancock)
Rock It (Herbie Hancock)
Shining Star (Earth, Wind and Fire)
Come Away with Me (Nora Jones)
Let's Stay Together (Al Green)
I Want You Back (Michael Jackson)
Shout it Out Loud (Prince)

Swing
Jump, Jive and Wail
Lady be Good
Choo Choo Ch'Boogie
Traffic Jam (Artie Shaw)
Everything is Jumping (Artie Shaw)
Juke Box Saturday Night (Glen Miller)

Latin—all by Tito Puente
El Cayuco
Que Sera Mi China (Colleccion Diamonte)
Oye Como Va (Carnival de Exitos)
Mambo Birdland (Mambo Birdland)
Cha Cha Cha Mambo (Mambo Birdland)
Chanchullo (Cocktail Hour)
Ron Kon Kan (Party with Puente)

<u>Oldies</u>
Night and Day
I Get a Kick Out of You
Let's Do It, Let's Fall in Love

Musical Selections for the Ceremony

Best Man and Ushers: Purcell's *Trumpet Tune in D*
Maid of Honor and Bridesmaids: Edward Elgar's *Salut d'Amour, Opus 12*
Groom: Clarke's *Prince of Denmark March*
Bride: *Intermezzo* from Mascagni's "Cavalleria Rusticana"

Other suggested selections:

Bach: Brandenburg Concerto #4, allegro
        Brandenburg Concerto #1 in F, first movement
        Brandenburg Concerto No.2, andante
        Air on a G String
Delibes: *Flower Duet* from "Lakme"
Greig: "Peer Gynt," Suite 1, Po.46 *Anitra's Dance*
Hayden: *Serenade*
Handel: *Arrival of the Queen of Sheba* from "Solomon"
Liszt: Nocturne #3 in A flat major (O Lieb so long du lieben kannst)
Mendelssohn: Canzonetta from Quartet, Op 12
Mouret: Rhondo (although it will recall *Masterpiece Theatre*)
Moussorgsky: Pictures at an Exhibition
Offenbach: *Barcarolle* from "Tales of Hoffman
Tchaikovsky: Theme from *Romeo and Juliet*
                Serenade for Strings, Op 48, First movement
Vivaldi: Concerto Gross in D Minor

Suggestions for the Recessional or Processional:
Bach: *Brandenburg Concerti*
Clarke: Prince of Denmark March
Dvorak: Carnival *Overture*
Handel: *Hornpipe* from "Water Music"
        Arrival of the Queen of Sheba
Mouret: Rondeau
Teleman: *Air de Trompette*

Appendix B

Bridal Salons in Manhattan

Clea Colet*
960 Madison Avenue
New York, NY 10021
212-396-4608

Amsale
625 Madison Avenue
New York, NY 10022
212-583-1700

Reem Acra
245 Seventh Avenue
New York, NY 10001
212-414-0980

Michele Roth
24 West 57th Street
New York, NY 10019
212-245-3390

Yumi Katsura
907 Madison Avenue
New York, NY 10021
212-772-3760

Vera Wang
991 Madison Avenue
New York, NY 10021
212-628-4300

Appendix C

Venues in Manhattan

The Mark Hotel*
Madison and 77th Street
New York, NY 10021
212-744-4300
www.madarinoriental.com

Manhattan Penthouse Suites
80 Fifth Avenue
New York, NY 10011
212-627-8838
www.mansioncatering.com

The Carlyle
Madison at 76th Street
New York, NN 10021
2122-744-1600
www.rosewoodhotels.com

W Hotels
541 Lexington Avenue
New York, NY 10022
212-4072903
www.whotels.com

Palm House at the Brooklyn Botanical Gardens
1000 Washington Avenue
Brooklyn, NY 11225
718-398-2400
www.palmhouse.com

The Pierre Hotel
Fifth Avenue at 61st Street
New York, NY 10021
212-838-8000
www.fourseasons.com

New York Historical Society
Dexter Hall and the Great Hall
170 Central Park West
New York, NY 10024
212-873-3400
www.nyhistory.org

St. Regis Hotel
2 East 55th Street
New York, NY 10022
212-753-4500
www.starwood.com

Appendix D

Services We Used

Venue
The Mark Hotel
77th Street at Madison Avenue
New York, NY 10021
212-744-4300
www.mandarinoriental.com

Cake
Sylvia Weinstock
373 Church Avenue
New York, NY 10013
212-925-6698
www.sylviaweinstock.com

Photographer
Rob Fraser Photography
rob@robfraser.com

Classical Music
Sterling Music Ensemble
Allegra Klein
345 East 93rd Street
New York, NY 10128
212-996-7565
www.sterlingmusic.com

Florist
Belle Fleur
11 East 27th Street
New York, NY 10010
212-254-8703
marilyn@bellefleur.com

Dress Designer
Rebeca SanAndres
81 Leonard Street
New York, NY 10013
212-278-1904

Bridemaids' Dresses
Serafina
25 West 36th Street
New York, NY 10018
212-253-2754

Invitations
Papyrus
Cynthia Magarit
1270 Third Avenue
New York, NY 212-717-1060

Jeweler
Wayne Haberman
579 Fifth Avenue
New York, NY 10017
212-944-2544

Veil and Tiara
Paul's Veils
28 West 38th Street
New York, NY 10018
212-391-3822

Appendix E

Budget Worksheet

Item   **Projected Cost**

food and beverage for dinner
@per person x number of guests
food and beverage for reception
(per person plus stations)
miscellaneous (coat check,
athroom attendant, etc.)
taxes

total _____

Stationery—Save-the-date cards
Wedding invitations/envelopes
Place Cards
Thank You Notes/envelopes

Total _____

Classical Music ....

Band...

Photographer..

Florist...

Wedding Gown...

Tuxedo...

Accessories for groom (shoes, cuff links, cummerbund and bow tie)... ....

Accessories for bride (shoes, bag, jewelry) ....

Veil and Tiara...

Beauty Services Hairstylist...

Make-up artist ....

Wedding bands ....

Officiant's fee ....

Limousine Service ....

Ketubah..

Yarmulkes...

Honeymoon (hotel and airfare)...

Grand Total_____

0-595-32739-7